HISTORICAL SOCIOLOGY: ITS ORIGINS AND DEVELOPMENT

Theories of Social Evolution from Cave Life to Atomic Bombing

BY

HARRY ELMER BARNES

PHILOSOPHICAL LIBRARY

NEW YORK

PRINTED IN THE UNITED STATES OF AMERICA

To
GEORGE A. LUNDBERG
Resolute Protagonist of
Scientific Method in Sociology

CONTENTS

CONTENTS

PREFACE

When, about a year ago, I wrote the preface to the *Introduction to the History of Sociology* I stated in good faith that the book constituted my final effort in the field of the history of social theory. But, shortly after this, I engaged to write a chapter on the development of historical sociology. It was quickly apparent that an adequate survey of this field would outrun the dimensions of any manageable chapter. Therefore, I decided to take such space as was required for at least a comprehensive introduction to the subject and to publish the results in book form.

The subject of historical sociology, and the contributions made to it through the ages from Plato to our day, has intrigued my interest since undergraduate days in college. It was the topic to which I gave most of my attention in graduate courses in sociology and anthropology. And considerable of my subsequent teaching was devoted to this theme.

This little book seeks to trace the rise of interest in the history of human society in classical times and its development since those days. It sets forth briefly the progress of attitudes, methods and interpretations, from the time of early evolutionary notions to the triumph of the scientific and empirical cultural approach to social origins and social evolution. Then comes a summary of what has actually been accomplished in contemporary writing in the field of historical sociology and what this has contributed to our knowledge of social and institutional development. The book concludes with some of the more practical applications of historical sociology to better social perspectives for our time and to a clearer understanding of the public problems of our age, as we move along in the great world-revolution of our era.

In relation to scholarship, the book endeavors to provide an introduction to the more important literature in the field and a guide to more fruitful writing therein during the years to come. In a practical way, it attempts to give the general reader some understanding of the character of the age in which we live, against the background of previous social eras, and to suggest some of the lessons involved for use in solving the dilemmas which encompass us. It is my hope, in the not distant future and with suitable collaboration, to prepare a systematic work on the actual history of human society, which, as this introductory survey makes clear, is the primary need in this field. The timbers have been gathered, but they have never been assembled in any complete and orderly structure

HARRY ELMER BARNES

Cooperstown, N. Y.
June 15, 1948.

PART ONE

*The Rise and Development of
Historical Sociology*

CHAPTER I

THE NATURE AND ORIGINS OF HISTORICAL SOCIOLOGY

I. PURPOSE AND SCOPE OF THIS BOOK

It is not my purpose in this book to set forth an exhaustive exposition and a detailed bibliographic summary of all the important contributions to every field of historical sociology. Rather, I shall attempt to select the chief typical tendencies and achievements in this branch of sociology, indicating the intellectual environments in which they arose, their significance in the sociological movement, and their defects. Incidentally, it will be a part of my plan to explain the relative decline of historical sociology in the last forty years and to indicate reasons for expecting its revival on a more extended scale and with a far more promising method and a more reliable body of fact and doctrine.

In our *Social Thought from Lore to Science* (Vol. I, Chap. XX), and our *Contemporary Social Theory* (Chaps. 2, 15) Professor Howard Becker has reviewed thoroughly the abstract and methodological aspects of the development of historical sociology. Hence I shall lay more stress on historical contributions and personal achievements.

II. THE FIELD AND PROVINCE OF HISTORICAL SOCIOLOGY

The field and province of historical sociology embrace a considerable scope and variety of interests and problems. Historical sociology seeks, in the first place, to account for the origins of associated life among human beings, here relying mainly upon data from anthropogeography, biology, and psychology.) It endeavors to trace the origins and development of all forms of social organization and social structures. It deals with the rise and evolution of all social institutions. It treats of the beginnings, domination and decline of those social attitudes and philosophies which have affected social activities in various stages of history. It examines the question of the stages in the evolution of social types and structures. It tries to discover and formulate the laws of social development, both with respect to broad stages of social evolution and with regard to particular periods and institutions. When it cannot discover laws of social evolution, it states the trends which are evident therein. It points out the historical basis of social maladjustments and social problems, laying special stress upon cultural lag or institutional maladjustment in our age. It takes up the problem of the elucidation and evaluation of the theory of social progress.

The question may be raised of the difference between the field of historical sociology and that of history, especially the so-called New History which treats of all phases of human life in the past. We shall not here go into the controversy as to whether history deals with the unique and never-repeated episodes of history and, hence, can never be a true social science. Historical sociologists and historians deal with the same data and periods of history. But the task of the historian is chiefly descriptive and concrete; in so far as he seeks to derive laws of historical development from his studies he becomes in reality a historical sociologist. If the historical sociologist deviates from his generalized search for laws and trends in the social development of mankind and goes in for purely descriptive exercises, he ceases thereby to function as a sociologist and assumes the rôle of a historian.

To illustrate by the history of the ancient Near East; both the historical sociologist and the historian deal with the pre-literary background of Egypt and Mesopotamia and review the human experience in Egypt, Sumeria, Baylonia, Chaldea, and Persia. But the historian is chiefly concerned with the life and daily activities of the peoples who inhabited these areas in antiquity. The sociologist considers the same data in order to discover the reasons for the passage from tribal to civil society and the social stages involved in this transition: the rise of tribal feudalism, the city-state, kingdoms and empires. He is interested in the rise, differentiation, and conflicts of social classes. He gives attention to the origins and development of the various organs of social control. He goes into the growth and mutation of the mores. He gives little space to purely descriptive materials except in so far as they may be used to illustrate institutional development.

Another problem is that of the relation between historical sociology and a genetic or evolutionary science of culture—culturology—as it is sometimes called. If we accept the now common tendency to regard culture as the complete complex of human beliefs, achievements, and institutions, then there is a very close resemblance between historical sociology and culturology, especially those phases of culturology which treat of institutional evolution. The two fields part company mainly when the culturologist ceases his concern with development and concentrates on the description of various forms of cultural achievement. Another incidental difference is that culturology has been mainly cultivated by anthropologists, though a considerable number of sociologists have recently contended that culture affords the best key to the understanding of social processes and have accepted something pretty close to a theory of cultural determinism.

Historical sociology was for many decades chiefly concerned

with the problems of social origins rather than with the general course of social evolution down to modern times. Hence, most works on historical sociology have dealt with primitive society. Therefore, there has been a close relationship and much over-lapping between historical sociology and anthropology. For this reason, much of any history of historical sociology must be occupied with the progress of methods and results in tracing the rise, nature and mutations of primitive social institutions. This also probably accounts for the fact that there is not in any language a comprehensive and unified treatment of the whole history of human society and social institutions from primitive times to the twentieth century.

III. THE ORIGINS AND DEVELOPMENT OF HISTORICAL SOCIOLOGY

In reviewing the contributions of the typical writers in historical sociology down to very recent times, the most striking fact which is likely to come to the attention of the student is the prevalence of a subjective attitude upon the part of the writers and the pursuance of the *a priori* method, in order to utilize the alleged facts of social development to substantiate some special doctrine of the writer or his school. From Plato until Vico, Hume, and Ferguson, if not to Boas and the critical anthropologists, one rarely discovers a writer on the history of human society who looked upon the development of society in an objective manner, with the avowed intention of discovering just what the nature of this process has been.

The beginnings of interest in, and reflection upon, the problems of social genesis go back to the rudimentary attempts to account for the allegedly unique and divine origin of the early civilizations. Familiar examples of this type of historical sociology are the Osiris Myth, the Gilgamesh Epic and its Hebrew appropriation in the Book of Genesis, and the numerous myths and epics of political derivation and genesis which flourished among the Greeks and Romans. The primitive foundations upon which these tales were constructed have been preserved for us in the creation myths of the uncivilized peoples of the present day.[1]

Perhaps the first group of thinkers who thoughtfully and rationally considered the problem of the origins of organized society were the Greek Sophists of the fifth century B.C.[2] They seem to have believed in an unregulated state of nature, which was ended when civil society was created through a governmental contract. One of the most complete and remarkable accounts of social genesis produced in ancient times was that set forth by Plato in Book III of his *Laws*. He assumed something of the chronological perspective of H. G. Wells when he stated that "every man should understand that the human race either had no beginning at all, and will never have an end, but will always be and has been, or that it began an immense while ago." He presented a somewhat Rousseauean picture of the felicity of the life of primitive peoples, and traced the gradual break-up of primitive society as it passed through the patriarchal period into civil society, which he clearly held to have been founded by means of a governmental contract.

Aristotle gave relatively little attention to the problems of social genesis, and his brief discussion of the matter was analytical rather than historical. He was chiefly concerned with demonstrating the social nature of man, and he traced the expanding expression of this social instinct in the family, village and the state. Some reliance on the historical and comparative method is to be discerned in his alleged study of some 158 constitutions as the basis of his *Constitution of Athens*.

One of the most neglected, and yet one of the most striking of the early discussions of social and political evolution is that contained in the sixth book of Polybius' *History of Rome*, in which he turned aside from his main theme to indicate the basic reasons for the supremacy of the Roman state.[3] He foreshadowed Bodin, Hume, Ferguson, and Gumplowicz by his doctrine that the state originated in force. He was in line with Sumner in expounding the customary basis of morality. Finally, he anticipated Spinoza, Hume, and Adam Smith by his discussion of reflective sympathy as a social force.

Infinitely the most realistic and satisfactory of classical theories of the history of society was that offered by the great Epicurean poet, Lucretius, in his effort to substantiate the evolutionary and naturalistic character of the development of the universe and society, independent of any aid or interference by the gods.[4] He held that material culture had passed through the sequence of Stone, Bronze and Iron Ages. He traced the origin of life, man, society, and the state, indicating the various stages of cultural and social evolution with astonishing accuracy. His remarkable *De rerum natura* was one of the most notable contributions to historical sociology down to the modern period. The Roman Stoic philosopher, Seneca, is significant for having carried even further than Plato the Rousseauean notion of the idyllic life of early man. He contended that man had originally lived in a golden age without avarice, sin, or crime until the appearance of private property. This produced jealousy, strife, and a general state of war and misery which made necessary the establishment of the state and civil society.

One of the most important results of the exposition of this doctrine by Seneca was its adaptation by the Christian Fathers to serve as the accepted Patristic view of the course of social evolution. The Fathers identified Seneca's "Golden Age" with the state of man before the "Fall" in Eden and held that the subsequent period of misery, confusion, and disorder was none other than that which followed the expulsion from Paradise. The establishment of the state, but more especially the coming of Christianity, served to make mundane existence more tolerable, though this life is but a preparation for the bliss of the elect of the City of God in the world to come.[5] This conception of the history of society prevailed through most of the Middle Ages, though the medieval writers often tended to overlook the alleged original felicity and to stress chiefly the miseries of existence before the establishment of the Christian polity.

The most remarkable contribution to historical sociology between Lucretius and Adam Ferguson was embodied in the *Prolegomena to Universal History* of the Muslim scholar and statesman, Ibn Khaldun (1332-1406).[6] He not only produced what is regarded by some as the first real philosophy of history, but also, in his description of Arabic society, contributed one of the best studies of primitive society down to the rise of modern anthropology. He also far surpassed Plato and Lucretius in tracing the stages in the evolution of human society and civilization.

In the latter part of the sixteenth century there appeared two important contributions to historical sociology in the writings of the French publicist, Jean Bodin, and of the Spanish Jesuit, Jean de Mariana.[7] Bodin distinguished carefully between society, which he believed developed naturally out of the social instinct, and the state, which he contended was a product of force and coercion. Mariana's view of social and political development was strangely like that of Seneca and Rousseau. Mankind had originally dwelt in a state of undisturbed happiness, but private property brought avarice, crime, and general disorder. It was found necessary to establish a superior civil power, which was accomplished by means of a governmental contract.

The most prevalent type of historical sociology during the seventeenth and eighteenth centuries was that which traced the evolution of society and the state through a social and a governmental contract.[8] The distinction between the social and the governmental contract was first clearly drawn by Aeneas Sylvius in the fifteenth century, and was still further elaborated by Richard Hooker at the end of the sixteenth. While such writers as Hobbes, Sydney, Spinoza, Locke, Pufendorf, Rousseau, and Kant employed the doctrine of the social contract to buttress quite different propositions in political theory and practice, they were generally agreed that man originally lived in a state of nature, from the miseries of which he escaped by means of an agreement of all to live an orderly existence in organized society (the social contract). Civil government was subsequently established through a governmental contract of the people with the ruler or rulers whom they had chosen. It is interesting to note, however, that the literal historicity of the social contract was not regarded as a vital point by many of its advocates. With Hobbes, Spinoza, Kant, and, to a lesser degree, with Rousseau, it was chiefly a logical assumption. One of the most significant results of this body of doctrine for historical sociology was Rousseau's highly imaginary and poetical eulogy of the "noble savage," living a carefree and paradisiacal existence, from which mankind had later been reduced to misery and chains by the development of culture, private property, and the state.

The historical and psychological errors of the social contract theory, as presented in its classic form, were attacked by three writers who may be said to have been the first to restore the historical point of view in sociology to the place it had held with Plato, Polybius, and Lucretius.[9] Giovanni Vico, while not devoting himself particularly to the demolition of the social contract, emphasized the necessity of pursuing an inductive and historical approach to social problems. The possibilities of such procedure he himself demonstrated in the fields of philology and jurisprudence. David Hume showed that the social contract theory was a logical fallacy, a psychological impossibility, and something which was refuted by the concrete facts of history.

He stressed the importance of the sex instinct, family cohesion and sympathy in the development of social relations, and contended that the state had its origin in force and owed its persistence to the gradual perception of its utility by mankind.

Even more modern in viewpoint was Adam Ferguson's *History of Civil Society* (1767). Ferguson stated the idea of the origin of the state in conquest and force so clearly that Ludwig Gumplowicz has claimed him as the first great exponent of this school of sociological thought. Further, he foreshadowed Boas and the critical school of anthropologists by insisting that we must discard preconceived hypotheses as to the nature of primitive man and his institutions, and study primitive society as it actually exists. If we do, said Ferguson, we shall find the situation far different from that pictured by such writers as Rousseau. Another interesting adumbration was his insistence that the current tendency to regard primitive man as widely different from modern man was highly misleading. While in his own works Ferguson may have fallen short of his canons of proper procedure in historical sociology, his discussion of method and attitudes was of real significance and surprisingly similar to our approach today.

The next impulse to historical sociology came from the philosophy of history and the history of civilization to which Vico was an early contributor.[10] Voltaire's *Essai sur les Moeurs,* Turgot's Sorbonne *Discourses,* Condorcet's *Esquisse d'un tableau historique des progrès de l'esprit humain,* and the works of Saint-Simon represent the more important early French contributions to this field, all marked by a greater or less degree of rationalism, skepticism, and optimism. In the works of Lessing, Herder, Schiller, Fichte, Schelling, and Hegel one finds, along with a gradually fading rationalism, the Romantic trend in the German philosophy of history, with its emphasis on national character, the indwelling of *Geist,* and distinctly mystic tendencies. Yet, with all its fantasies, the Romantic impulse was, as Lord Acton has well insisted, remarkable for the scope of the historical interests which it stimulated. The history of politics, law, art, religion, and language owed much to the impulse derived from Romanticism. In the work of Auguste Comte rationalism and Romanticism of a French brand were combined to furnish the historical background of the first formal system of sociological doctrine. Comte's notion of the main stages in social evolution will be described later on. While there is little doubt that historical sociology is something considerably different in method and content from the philosophy of history, yet, in its attempt to find some meaning and significance in the flow of events in the past, the philosophy of history contributed much in the way of both impulse and data to the development of historical sociology.

No little importance must also be assigned to the rise of critical historical scholarship in the work of Leopold von Ranke and his disciples and students in many countries.[11] While there was little sociological orientation or interest in the most of the scientific history of the nineteenth century, yet, by improving the mechanism of research, it did much to advance and refine the inductive method of approach to historical sociology and it brought forth a large amount of concrete material which has either been utilized or still awaits exploitation by the historical sociologist.

While prehistoric archeology, systematic ethnology and anthropology mainly flourished after the rise of evolutionary doctrine and were nourished and stimulated by it, these fields of knowledge, so indispensable to historical sociology, were definitely established in pre-Darwinian days.[12] William Buckland, Vedel Simonsen, Christian J. Thomsen, J. J. A. Worsaae, and Jacques Boucher de Perthes founded prehistoric archeology in the period before the publication of *The Origin of Species.*

Gustav Klemm (1802–1867) appropriated and interpreted this work to create the first systematic work on the cultural history of man, his *Allgemeine Cultur-geschichte der Menschheit* (1843–1855). Comparative anthropology of a pre-evolutionary variety was founded by Franz Theodor Waitz (1821–1864) in his six-volume *Anthropologie der Naturvölker* (1858–1871), which laid special stress on primitive mental patterns and racial traits. Even Adolf Bastian (1826–1905), author of the famous and influential *Der Mensch in der Geschichte* (1859, 3 vols.), who provided the classical evolutionary anthropologists with one of their fundamental tenets, the doctrine of parallel cultural development based on the hypothesis of the uniformity of the human mind the world over, did not accept the application of Darwinian conceptions to human culture.

The last of the pre-evolutionary and pre-Darwinian impulses which may be said to have influenced the development of historical sociology was the initial interest in historical economics and economic history evident in the work of Heeren, Sismondi, List, Marx, Hildebrand, Roscher and Knies.[13] The genetic point of view, the breadth of interests, and concern with social reform which characterized the group brought them exceedingly close to the borders of historical sociology.

Unquestionably the most potent influences contributing to the rise and development of truly historical sociology were Spencer's theory of cosmic evolution and the Darwinian doctrine of organic evolution, and their reaction upon social science. These conceptions provided concrete and convincing evidence to substantiate the brilliant intuition of Lucretius and the ancient evolutionists, and implied that human society, as well as organic life, is the natural product of evolutionary forces operating over an immense period of time. While many grotesque errors grew out of the attempt to carry biological formulas directly over into sociology, and much effort was wasted in drawing far-fetched analogies between biological and social structures and processes, the evolutionary impulse was unquestionably the force that put historical sociology, in its contemporary manifestations, thoroughly upon its feet. It followed two major lines of development—the social Darwinism of Gumplowicz and his school, and the evolutionary and comparative anthropology of Herbert Spencer, J. F. McLennan, John Lubcock, Andrew Lang, James G. Frazer, Charles J. M. Letourneau, J. J. Bachofen, Albert Hermann Post, Daniel G. Brinton, and Lewis Henry Morgan. Both of these lines of development will be touched on later in this book and need not be further described at this point.

What may be narrowly and technically described as the systematic historical sociology of the last third of the nineteenth century was both created by, and based upon, the evolutionary anthropology of the writers just mentioned. This is particularly apparent not only in such general works as those of Spencer and Morgan but also in such special treatises as those by Edward Westermarck on the history of the family. The most masterly synthesis of historical sociology produced at the time, Book III of Franklin Henry Giddings' *Principles of Sociology* (1896), was based essentially both upon the method and the data of the evolutionary school, as, indeed, it had to be when written.

While the critical historico-analytical anthropology of Franz Boas and his disciples in this country and of Robert R. Marett, Paul Max Ehrenreich, and others in Europe has provided a new and far sounder method for studying social evolution, and has destroyed many of the conclusions of both comparative anthropology and the earlier historical sociology, it has been but little appropriated for historical sociology. The primary reason for this is probably the fact that interest in historical sociology, which was, perhaps, ascendant before 1900, has declined to a surprising degree in the twentieth century, especially in the United States. Hence, sociology has provided few sociologists who have been interested in reconstructing our knowledge of social evolution on the basis of the newer methods and more assured results of the critical anthropology. It is not without significance that the first real attempts to indicate the significance of scientific anthropology for a reliable history of society have been executed by professional anthropologists such as Marett, Clark Wissler, Robert H. Lowie, Alexander A. Goldenweiser, A. L. Kroeber and Richard Thurnwald.

1. See A. L. Kroeber and T. T. Waterman, *Source Book in Anthropology* (Berkeley: University of California Press, 1920), pp. 516ff; and J. O. Hertzler, *The Social Thought of the Ancient Civilizations* (New York: McGraw-Hill, 1936).
2. On the Greek contributions, see Ernest Barker, *Greek Political Thought* (New York: Macmillan, 1919, 2 vols.).
3. H. E. Barnes and Howard Becker, *Social Thought from Lore to Science* (Boston: D. C. Heath, 1938, 2 vols.), Vol. I, pp. 197–200.
4. *Ibid.*, pp. 200–202.
5. *Ibid.*, Chap. VI.
6. Nathaniel Schmidt, *Ibn Khaldun,* (New York: Columbia University Press, 1930).
7. Barnes and Becker, *op. cit.,* pp. 338–339, 348–358, 438–439.
8. G. P. Gooch, *Political Ideas from Bacon to Halifax* (New York; Holt, 1915); and H. J. Laski, *Political Thought from Locke to Bentham* (New York: Holt, 1920).
9. Barnes and Becker, *op. cit.,* pp. 396–411, 465–470, 451–452, 545–546; and W. C. Lehman, *Adam Ferguson and the Beginnings of Modern Sociology* (New York: Columbia University Press, 1930).
10. H. E. Barnes, *History of Historical Writing* (Norman: University of Oklahoma Press, 1930).
11. *Ibid.*, Chap. X.
12. R. H. Lowie, *The History of Ethnological Theory* (New York: Farrar and Rinehart, 1938), Chaps. I–II; and A. C. Haddon, *A History of Anthropology* (New York: Putnam, 1910), Chaps. VIII, XII.
13. J. K. Ingram, *A History of Political Economy* (New York: Macmillan, 1894), Chap. VI; and A. W. Small, *Origins of Sociology* (Chicago: University of Chicago Press, 1924), Chap. XI.

CHAPTER II

DARWINISM, EVOLUTIONARY OR COMPARATIVE ANTHROPOLOGY, AND HISTORICAL SOCIOLOGY

I. THE CONTRIBUTIONS OF DARWINISM TO HISTORICAL SOCIOLOGY

One need not concern himself especially with the history of method in sociology before the entry of the Darwinian concepts, for, with few exceptions, the method was deductive or intuitive. Even what little study was made of concrete data was usually for the purpose of substantiating some preconceived scheme of social evolution, such as the social contract. In the case of Ibn Khaldun one finds something of an inductive approach, but even in such instances as those of Lucretius and Khaldun the soundness of their generalizations was in large part the product of brilliant intuition.

The first important effect of Darwinism upon historical sociology was the impulse which it gave to the attempt to carry over directly the assumptions and formulas of evolutionary biology into an explanation of social evolution, without making the modifications that were necessary in view of the many and important differences in the type of data being analyzed.[1] This line of approach, generally known as Social Darwinism, was usually combined with a rather complete acceptance of evolutionary and comparative anthropology, thus adding to the specific errors of Social Darwinism those involved in evolutionary anthropology, which we shall examine later on in dealing with writers like Spencer and Morgan. Outstanding examples

16

of Social Darwinism were Ludwig Gumplowicz's *Rasse und Staat, Der Rassenkampf,* and *Grundriss der Soziologie;* Gustav Ratzenhofer's *Wesen und Zweck der Politik,* and *Soziologie;* and Franz Oppenheimer's *Der Staat* (which was revised and enlarged as the second volume of his *System der Soziologie*). While such writers, especially Gumplowicz (1838–1909), were guilty of many errors in methodology, their contention that the state and political society came into being as the result of a long series of conquests, the subsequent amalgamation of social groups, and the assimilation of cultural traits is regarded as probably the most important sociological contribution to the clarification of political origins.

Gumplowicz's conception of political origins and evolution may be summarized as follows: [2] The human race may be assumed to have had a polygenetic origin (i.e. differentiated from the parent simian stock in many places over the planet). This led to the apparance of many different and heterogeneous social groups. These groups were led into conflict with each other through the natural and inevitable tendency of all individuals and groups to seek to improve their economic well-being and to increase the material means of satisfying their desires. The earliest conquests of one group by another usually led to the extermination of the conquered; but, sooner or later, slaughter was commuted into physical and political subjugation. In this manner arose the state and political sovereignty.

These primordial political societies soon became complicated by the development of social, economic, and religious classes, each called into existence to meet some definite social need. The processes of conflict, which had earlier taken the form of intergroup conquests, then became transformed into class conflicts within the state. This intragroup conflict led gradually to an amalgamation and assimilation of the diverse elements, con-

flicting classes and contending interests within the state and
to the emancipation of the masses. When this process was
carried to completion it brought into being the folk-state or
nation, which is the final and supreme product of social
evolution.

But intergroup conflict was not terminated by the creation of
the folk-state. Gumplowicz agreed with Machiavelli that the
state has an inevitable tendency to expand or decline. Hence,
one folk-state attempts to conquer other folk-states, and the
processes of warfare, conflict, amalgamation and assimilation
are repeated. No limit can be set to the possible or desirable
expansion of folk-states. The natural tendency is for a state to
increase until its strength fails through either successful re-
sistance by its enemies or internal corruption and disruption.
The tenets of individual morality have no relation whatever to
the conduct of states in their process of expansion. The state is
a product of nature and is ruled and guided by natural laws
which remove its acts from the realm of conventional ethical
judgments.

Gumplowicz's fellow Austrian sociologist, Gustav Ratzenhofer (1842–1904), was deeply influenced by the former's
doctrine of political origins through physical conquest.[3] But
Ratzenhofer was more concerned with the later struggles between classes within the state than with the earlier conflicts
between groups which gave rise to the origin of the state. The
absolute hostility of all men and social groups to each other in
the state of nature leads to conflict and conquest. This results
in the evolution of what Ratzenhofer calls the conquest-state,
and he agrees rather completely with Gumplowicz's doctrine of
the origin of the state.

This emergence of the conquest-state ended kinship society
and created political institutions. From this point onward, the
chief political process is the evolution of what Ratzenhofer

designates as the "culture-state." It originates in systematic political domination and subordination at the hands of rulers. But, in time, the state assumes the rôle of a mediator in the conflicts within the state—of the umpire of the social process. This assures a balance of power among the various interests within the state. In this way, the culture-state combines the essential dominion of law and order, through political subordination, with the provision of creative cultural freedom. The most perfect type of state which has thus far been produced is one in which the political authorities maintain the best possible balancing of governmental control with cultural strivings and thus assure the most complete functioning of the contesting interest-groups within the state.

The conception of political origins set forth by Franz Oppenheimer (1864–1943) was similar to the ideas of Gumplowicz and Ratzenhofer, but Oppenheimer's interest in political and social evolution was subordinate to his basic concern with the evolution of what he regarded as the fundamental social evil of land monopoly and with its ultimate solution through rural coöperative societies.[4]

Oppenheimer repudiated any complete reliance on the old evolutionary anthropology and admitted the possibility of the diffusion of institutional patterns and cultural traits. He held that primitive hunters and Neolithic horticulturalists lived in a state of relative economic equality, free from land monopoly, conquest, private property, and any hierarchy of social classes. The first great period of physical conquest came during the Bronze Age, when groups of pastoral nomads entered upon an era of aggression and subjected other groups to their political control. This produced the state, according to the same formula as that suggested by Gumplowicz and Ratzenhofer. But what interested Oppenheimer more than the origin of the state was the fact that, in the process of creating the state through conquest, the evils of private property, land monopoly, economic inequality, and a hierarchy of social classes were also produced.

Oppenheimer traced the evolution of political institutions and land monopoly through the course of Roman and medieval history—through the growth of the *Latifundia* and the medieval manors—to the rise of the national state in modern times. He found some improvement in the manorial period, where the peasantry had a sort of elementary coöperative organization. While the national state tended to displace the political institutions and legal authority of the feudal system, it did not wipe out land monopoly or emancipate the peasantry, this failure being the most important cause of the French Revolution. Even the development of representative government and democracy in the nineteenth and twentieth centuries failed to end land monopoly, which continues to be the chief cause of, and instrument for, the exploitation of the masses. The solution is to be found in the establishment of rural producer-coöperatives which will end land monopoly and make possible social justice, to promote which was the fundamental purpose of Oppenheimer in all his main works on sociology.

The doctrines of Gumplowicz and Ratzenhofer were warmly espoused in the United States. Lester F. Ward was greatly impressed with Gumplowicz's notion of the origin of the state and fully adopted it in his *Pure Sociology* (1903). Ratzenhofer's conception of the culture-state, devoted to promoting the constructive conflict and adjustment of social interests within the state, was enthusiastically embraced by Albion W. Small in his *General Sociology* (1905), and by Arthur F. Bentley in his *The Process of Government* (1908). Oppenheimer's historical attack on land monopoly engaged the interest of our agrarian reformers, but his sane program for a solution of the problem through rural producer-coöperatives prevented American

"Single-Taxers" from espousing any complete acceptance of his ideas.

Another, and a more direct and logical application of Darwinian principles to social evolution consisted in the effort to discover just how far the Darwinian formulas of biological evolution are valid in the field of cultural and institutional evolution. Perhaps the most straight-forward attempt to do this was made by Professor Albert Galloway Keller (1874–). Keller addressed his work on *Societal Evolution* (1915) to the following question: "Can the evolutionary theory . . . be carried over into the social domain without losing all or much of the significance it possesses as applied in the field of natural science?" Keller holds that, so far as the formula of evolution has been adopted by sociologists, it has been the doctrine of cosmic evolution elaborated by Spencer, which, he thinks, is not a scientific but a philosophic concept. Hence, it is high time that the really scientific formulas of Darwin should be appropriated by sociology, and the doctrine of the "transformation of the incoherent homogeneous into the coherent heterogeneous" be displaced by that of "variation, selection, transmission, and adaptation." If it is true, as Keller attempts to prove, that the Darwinian doctrine is applicable, with qualifications, to social processes, the question arises as to how far society can control this evolutionary process and artificially improve social institutions, as breeders improve the stock of animals by artificial selection.

In the first place, Keller finds that societal evolution is primarily mental and institutional, not physical. The conception of the "mores" developed by Sumner is the basis of Keller's theory of societal evolution. By the mores is meant the ways of doing things which a particular society approves. The mores are analogous to the germ cells and embryos in the organic world;

they are the "raw material" through which societal evolution operates.

Keller next proceeds to inquire as to whether the main factors in the Darwinian theory of evolution—variation, selection, transmission and adaptation—are exemplified in the evolution of the mores. He believes that they are.

Variation in the mores is shown by the fact that no two groups possess identical codes of customary procedure. These variations arise from the differences among groups in their responses to the stimulation of their environment.

Keller finds three types of societal selection—automatic, rational, and counter-selection. Automatic selection involves no conscious adaptation of means to a preconceived end, but is effected spontaneously through the processes of war, subjection, class conflict, and competition. He has some harsh, but in the main justifiable, words for those who would put an end to this natural process of the elimination of the socially unfit:

Sentimentalists, warm of heart, but soft of head, petition complaisant executives to let loose upon society the wolves that have been trapped and should have been eliminated once for all; to set the scotched snakes free again. The pseudo-heroic and pathetic aspects of the life of the black-hearted criminal are rehearsed until he seems to be a martyr, and the just judge who condemns him a persecutor and a brute. All of which is done by volatile spirits under the illusion that they are thereby conserving the delicacy of the "ethical sense" or what not, instead of proving recreant to plain duties as members and supporters of civilized society.[5]

Rational selection, the social analogue of the breeder's art, takes place in society, but in different degrees among the various types of mores. Those mores connected with matters of superstition and sentiment, like religion and sex, are most difficult to change by deliberate effort. Those not thus entangled open a wider field for conscious improvement. To a certain extent, the leaders in thought can determine the direction in which changes in the mores will occur, but even such persons are limited by the tyranny of public opinion.

Mores connected with the maintenance of society—industry—are the least wrapped up in sentiment, and hence rational selection finds its widest application in the economic field. Every important change in economic organization is followed by a consequent, though not necessarily equal, transformation in the other mores. Many changes can, thus, be achieved in this roundabout manner. Therefore, Keller's answer to the question as to whether society can control its own evolution ends in a new version of economic determinism. He guards, however, against allowing his arguments to be interpreted as favoring socialist propaganda. One may accept the dogma of the fundamental importance of economic institutions without giving assent to the Marxian deductions from this principle.

By counter-selection, Keller means that type of societal selection which renders the human race biologically less fit. The modern social factors in counter-selection, which are described by Friedrich Wilhelm Schallmayer, are mainly war, modern industry, celibacy, later marriage, and the sterility of the upper classes. But counter-selection, while disastrous biologically, may have social and cultural compensations. Societal selection operates primarily upon groups rather than individuals, and hence, in so far as it secures social advantages which are greater than the biological loss, it is to be commended. Keller regards the eugenics program advanced by Galton and Pearson as impracticable, since it involves interference with a type of mores—the sexual—which are very resistant to rational control.

Transmission, in sociological terminology, is not possible in the sense of biological heredity, but the mores can be transmitted through the medium of tradition, which operates automatically through imitation and inheritance, and artificially through education.

Adaptation in the mores is the outcome of the operation of the processes of variation, selection, and transmission. Every social custom or institution is the result of an adaptation of the life of a people to the environmental conditions which confront them. Even though any particular adjustment may later become an anachronism, it should not be condemned absolutely, for it must have once been useful or it would not have existed for long. The different forms of government are but one aspect of this social adaptation to the necessary conditions of social existence.

Keller thus demonstrates the applicability of the Darwinian formulas to the processes of social evolution in a broad, general way. It is debatable, however, whether we can find any real explanation of the fundamental social processes in a demonstration of the resemblances between the life processes of the organism and society.

Another phase of Social Darwinism was manifested in the writings of what we know of as the Organismic School of sociologists, especially, Herbert Spencer (1820–1903), Paul von Lilienfeld (1829–1903), Albert G. F. Schäffle (1831–1903), and René Worms (1869–1926). These writers were mainly interested in elaborating the alleged similarities or identities between the nature and processes of a human society and the biological organism. They produced voluminous treatises, but made no great contribution to historical sociology. Their works touched the latter chiefly in indicating that the growth of social structures may be very similar to the development of the organism. They implied that a society, like the organism, tends to grow, flourish, decline and wither away. In this way, they offered socio-biological confirmation of the old cyclical theory of social development.

II. THE REACTION OF EVOLUTIONARY OR COMPARATIVE
ANTHROPOLOGY ON HISTORICAL SOCIOLOGY

As influential and characteristic of the social science of this period as outright Social Darwinism was the rise of what is known as evolutionary or comparative anthropology, which colored the nature and conclusions of historical sociology for a generation or more during the last third of the nineteenth century and the opening of the twentieth. Writers of this school of evolutionary thought contended that there is an organic law of development and progress in social institutions. The theory of unilateral evolutionary growth was adhered to, along with its implications of gradual and orderly changes, much the same the world over, and, in general, proceeding from simple and confused relations to complex and well-coördinated social adjustments. On account of the assumed unity of the human mind all over the world, as suggested by Herder, Waitz and Bastian, and similarities in the geographical environment, it was held that we must expect parallelisms in cultural and institutional evolution among peoples widely separated in their geographic distribution. Finally, it was considered valid, in reconstructing the record of social development, to link together a series of isolated examples of any type of culture, drawn from the most diverse regions and periods of time and irrespective of the totality of the cultural complex from which each was taken, in a prearranged scheme of evolution. It was held that the results obtained from this method would reveal the actual course of social evolution and cultural growth.[6]

Among sociologists who espoused the evolutionary and comparative method Herbert Spencer was unquestionably the one who accepted it in its most extreme form and the one whose writings have been most influential. Spencer's work in social evolution fell into three phases or types. As an evolutionist, he interpreted social evolution as an aspect of cosmic evolution, following his well-known formula of the integration of matter and differentiation of form. As a member of the Organicist school, he portrayed social development in accord with the alleged laws of organic growth and development. As an evolutionary anthropologist he thoroughly accepted the basic principles of the comparative method. We are here concerned with this third aspect of Spencer's social evolutionism, that based on the comparative method of evolutionary anthropology. Spencer's somewhat naïve description or, perhaps better, confession, of his method of procedure in tracing social evolution by the comparative method is outlined in the following passage from his *Autobiography:*

With the entry of this new division of my work, the marshalling of evidence became a much more extensive and complicated business than it had hitherto been. The facts, so multitudinous in their numbers, so different in their kinds, so varied in their sources, formed a heterogeneous aggregate difficult to bring into the clear and effective order required for carrying on an argument; so that I felt much as might a general of a division who had become commander-in-chief; or rather, as one who had to undertake this highest function in addition to the lower functions of all his subordinates of the first, second, and third grades. Only by deliberate method persistently followed, was it possible to avoid confusion. A few words may fitly be said here concerning my materials, and the ways in which I dealt with them.

During the five and twenty preceding years there had been in course of accumulation, extracts and memoranda from time to time made. My reading, though not extensive, and though chiefly devoted to the subjects which occupied me during this long interval, frequently brought under my eyes note-worthy facts bearing on this or that division of Sociology. These, along with the suggested ideas, were jotted down and put away. The resulting mass of manuscript materials remained for years unclassified; but every now and then I took out the contents of the drawer which received these miscellaneous contributions and put them in some degree of order

—grouping together the ecclesiastical, the political, the industrial, etc.; so that by the time I began to build, there had been formed several considerable heaps of undressed stones and bricks.

But I now had to utilize the relatively large masses of materials gathered together in the *Descriptive Sociology*. For economization of labor, it was needful still further to classify these; and to save time, as well as to avoid errors in re-transcription, my habit was, with such parts of the work as were printed, to cut up two copies. Suppose the general topic to be dealt with was "Primitive Ideas." Then the process was that of reading through all the groups of extracts concerning the uncivilized and semi-civilized races under the head of "Superstition," as well as those under other heads that were likely to contain allied evidence—"Knowledge," "Ecclesiastical," etc. As I read I marked each statement that had any significant bearing; and these marked statements were cut out by my secretary after he had supplied any reference which excision would destroy. The large heap resulting was joined with the kindred heap of materials previously accumulated; and there now came the business of re-classifying them all in preparation for writing. During a considerable preceding period the subdivisions of the topic of "Primitive Ideas" had been thought about; and various heads of chapters had been settled—"Ideas of Sleep and Dreams," "Ideas of Death and Resurrection," "Ideas of Another Life," "Ideas of Another World," etc. etc. Taking a number of sheets of double foolscap, severally fitted to contain between their two leaves numerous memoranda, I placed these in a semi-circle on the floor round my chair; having indorsed each with the title of a chapter, and having arranged them in something like proper sequence. Then, putting before me the heap of extracts and memoranda, I assigned each as I read it to its appropriate chapter. Occasionally I came upon a fact which indicated to me the need for a chapter I had not thought of. An additional sheet for this was introduced, and other kindred facts were from time to time placed with this initial one. Several sittings were usually required to thus sort the entire heap. Mostly too, as this process was gone through some time in advance of need, there came a repetition, or several repetitions, before the series of chapters had assumed its final order, and the materials had all been distributed.

When about to begin a chapter, I made a further rough classification. On a small table before me I had a large rude desk—a hinged board, covered with green baize, which was capable of being inclined at different angles by a movable prop behind. Here I grouped the collected materials appropriate to the successive sections of the chapter; and those which were to be contained in each section were put into the most convenient sequence. Then, as I dictated, I from time to time handed to my secretary an extract to be incorporated.[7]

Goldenweiser has well summarized the shortcomings of this procedure: "The principal error of the evolutionists consisted in the fact that their alleged series of historical stages were made up of links drawn from the most varied times and places. These links were not in themselves bits of development, but static cross-cuts of a culture at the point of a particular rite, belief or custom. These static links were then put together end to end, making up what was claimed to be an historical series of stages." [8]

From the standpoint of methodology and evolutionary generalizations and their influence upon historical sociology, much the most important book turned out by the evolutionary school was Lewis Henry Morgan's *Ancient Society,* published in 1877.[9] Morgan (1818–1881) was a wealthy and cultivated American lawyer and business man who devoted himself industriously to a study of anthropology and formulated a famous scheme of social evolution. Unlike men like Spencer, Frazer and Letourneau, Morgan actually spent considerable time in the field, where he studied primitive life and institutions with much insight and ability. It was Morgan's contention that human institutions follow a definite pattern of evolution and that their stages of development are much the same the world over. This uniformity of evolution he attributed to the general similarity of basic human wants and the underlying unity of the human mind:

The history of the human race is one in source, one in experience and one in progress . . . inventions and discoveries show . . . the unity of the origin of mankind, the similarity of human wants in the same stage of advancement, and the uniformity of the operations of the human mind in similar conditions of society. . . . The principal institutions of mankind have been developed from a few primary germs of thought; . . . the course and manner of their development was predetermined, as well as restricted within narrow limits of divergence by the natural logic of the human mind and the necessary limitations of its powers. Progress has been found to be substantially the same in kind in tribes and nations inhabiting different and even disconnected continents, while in the same status, with the deviations from uniformity in particular instances produced by special causes . . . the experience of mankind has run in nearly uniform channels; human necessities in similar conditions have been substantially the same and the operations of the mental principle have been uniform in virtue of the specific identity of the brain of all the races of mankind. . . .

Like the successive geological formations, the tribes of mankind may be arranged, according to their relative conditions, into successive strata. When thus arranged, they reveal with some degree of certainty the entire range of human progress from savagery to civilization. A thorough study of each successive stratum will develop whatever is special in its culture and characteristics and yield a definite conception of the whole, in their difference and their relations. . . .[10]

Following out his general evolutionary scheme, Morgan held that culture has everywhere passed through three stages; savagery, barbarism, and civilization. During the periods of savagery and barbarism there were three stages of development within each. The lowest stage of savagery lasted from the beginning of the human race to the acquisition of a fish subsistence and a knowledge of the use of fire. These achievements introduced the middle stage of savagery. This continued until man invented the bow and arrow, which brought him into the upper stage of savagery. Man attained the stage of barbarism with the invention of the art of pottery. This entitled him to rank in the lower stage of barbarism. When man learned to domesticate animals in the Old World, to cultivate corn in the New World, and to build abodes of brick and stone he entered upon the middle stage of barbarism. When he learned how to smelt iron and to use iron tools and weapons, he emerged into the upper stage of barbarism. He entered civilization when he invented a phonetic alphabet, and created a government based upon territory and property rather than upon tribal relationships.

In his doctrine of social evolution, Morgan held that mankind had originally lived in small and unorganized hordes. Next, man entered what Morgan called gentile society, based upon real or alleged blood relationship. In its earliest form, this relationship was traced through mothers, thus creating a maternal society. In time, relationships were traced primarily through the fathers, and a patriarchal type of society came about. When government came to be based upon territorial residence and provided for the possession and transmission of property, the era of kinship or gentile society came to an end and civil society arose.

Morgan not only set forth a general theory of social evolution, but he also expounded doctrines relative to the evolution of particular institutions such as the family. He held that the family had passed through a number of forms. The first was the consanguine family, in which brothers and sisters married. The next type was the punaluan, which was designed to prevent the intermarriage of brothers and sisters by imposing a taboo thereupon by means of kinship organization—what the Scotch legal historian, McLennan, called the institution of exogamy. Then came the third or syndyasmian family, which was a marriage of single pairs but without exclusive cohabitation. The fourth form of family was the patriarchal family, consisting of the marriage of one man to several wives and of male dominion. Finally, man attained the fifth and highest form of marriage, the monogamous, which meant the marriage of one man to one woman with exclusive cohabitation. This last form was encouraged by the rise of property and its legal transmission to offspring.

No other book ever published in the field of social science has exerted so great an influence upon our ideas regarding the evolution of social institutions as did Morgan's *Ancient Society*. For a generation it was the bible of anthropologists and sociologists. In the twentieth century, however, more critical anthropologists, led by Boas and his disciples, have severely criticized Morgan's ideas and have claimed that his notion of an invariable and inevitable sequence in social evolution does not square with observed facts. Perhaps the most complete attempt to refute Morgan is contained in Robert H. Lowie's *Primitive Society* (1920). On the other hand, Professor Leslie A. White, an admirer of Morgan, is now undertaking to rehabilitate Morgan's general conception of social evolution, without necessarily approving all of Morgan's specific notions.[11]

Whatever the deficiencies in the details of Morgan's theory of social evolution, the dynamic element in it is of permanent value. This rests upon the contention that culture advances and institutions change as the technological items in man's control over his environment are enlarged and improved. We have noted how Morgan related the stages in human progress from savagery to civilization directly to the progress in weapons, tools, the use of metals, types of abodes, and the domestication of animals. Morgan also made a contribution of great value in showing how profoundly social evolution has been affected by the institution of property and the methods of transmitting it through inheritance practices. Morgan's stress upon technological and economic elements in institutional change and readjustment is sound and of vital importance. Of the greatest permanent importance, however, was Morgan's conception that human culture and institutions represent an evolutionary process of development. This is the vital item, and critical anthropology has not overthrown this contention of Morgan and his fellow evolutionists, however much devastation it has wrought with respect to the specific evolutionary dogmas and patterns of Morgan and his generation. The enduring value of *Ancient Society* has often been overlooked by critics who have concentrated upon less important aspects of Morgan's evolutionary philosophy and system and upon errors in matters of detail. Morgan's emphasis on technological and economic factors in social evolution has made his ideas especially acceptable to Marxians, and his work is today highly esteemed in Soviet Russia, long after his methodology has been discarded by most anthropologists and historical sociologists.

Other American works illustrating the application of evolutionism to primitive culture were J. W. Powell's work on social organization; F. H. Cushing's contributions to primitive mythology and material culture; Otis T. Mason's books on primitive industry; W. J. McGee's writings on primitive mentality and knowledge; and Daniel G. Brinton's books on early mentality and religion.

Perhaps the most extreme and uncritical exemplification of the unilineal evolutionary anthropology and historical sociology was contained in the numerous works of the French writer, Charles J. M. Letourneau (1831–1904). He summarized his ideas and findings in his *La Sociologie d'après l'ethnologie* (1892), and applied the evolutionary method to the development of nearly all forms of institutional growth and cultural manifestations. Representative of his studies are: *L'Évolution de la propriété* (1889); *L'Évolution de la morale* (1887); *L'Évolution politique* (1890); *L'Évolution jurique* (1891); and

La Condition de la femmes dans les diverses races et civilisations (1903). His books are probably the most voluminous and naïve exhibit of evolutionary anthropology and sociology.

Running a close second to Letourneau in his forthright and uncritical evolutionism and surely the most prolific writer and compiler of all the evolutionary anthropologists was Sir James George Frazer (1854–1941), the English classical scholar and evolutionary anthropologist.[12] Frazer devoted his studies chiefly to the evolution of religious institutions and ideas and mythology, but he also gave some attention to the early history of politics and primitive material culture. Frazer's more important books were *The Golden Bough,* which first appeared in 1900 and in many later and successively enlarged editions; *Lectures on the Early History of the Kingship* (1905); *Psyche's Lamp*; a *Discourse concerning the Influence of Superstition on the Growth of Institutions* (1919); *Totemism and Exogamy* (1910); *The Magic Art and the Evolution of Kings* (1911); *The Belief in Immortality and the Worship of the Dead* (1913–1924); *Folklore in the Old Testament* (1918); and *Myths of the Origin of Fire* (1930).

Frazer's methodology was that of the slips-of-paper compilation, so clearly and naïvely outlined by Spencer and Westermarck. He assembled a vast amount of descriptive material, which was as good as the sources which he used rather uncritically. Frazer wrote in an engaging and eloquent style and his *Golden Bough,* which was his main contribution to the evolution of religious ideas and institutions, has been probably the most widely read of all the books turned out by the evolutionary school. While it helped greatly to upset orthodox views of religious origins, and was thus an important contribution to the secularization of religious and social thought, this work, like the rest of Frazer's books, was in a methodological sense only a gigantic exhibit of uncritical evolutionism in its least inhibited manifestations. The most detailed and devastating revelation of the unreliability of Frazer's methods and conclusions was carried out in Goldenweiser's analysis of Frazer's *Totemism and Exogamy* in the former's doctoral dissertation, *Totemism: an Analytical Study* (1910). Perhaps the most misleading dogma which Frazer passed over to historical sociology and cultural history was his notion that primitive magic provided the basis of science. Closely resembling Frazer's evolutionary approach to religion were Andrew Lang's *Myth, Ritual and Religion* (1887); E. S. Hartland's *Ritual and Belief* (1914); A. E. Crawley's *The Tree of Life* (1905); and Frank Byron Jevons' popular *Introduction to the History of Religion* (1896).

There is often a tendency to go from one extreme to another in social thought, and this was well exemplified in the case of the hypercritical attitude towards social evolutionism. The latter practically dominated the field of anthropological and sociological thought for a half century after 1860. Then, when the critical anthropologists had shattered the dogmatic scheme of social evolution which the older evolutionists had worked out, there was an inclination to discard the whole idea of social evolution and to deny any validity in the notion. But the judicious members of the critical school, such as Goldenweiser, have pointed out the grave mistake in any such complete repudiation. The contributions of the evolutionists were of great and enduring value for social science. They were the first to provide a scientific explanation of human and social development and to show that naturalistic causes control social evolution. They were the first to introduce into social science the evolutionary, developmental and genetic point of view which is a cornerstone of contemporary social science. This they did in a generation when the historians showed scarcely any interest in, or conception of, social and institutional genesis. As James Harvey Robinson pointed out at the turn of the century, few social scientists were less historical-minded at that time than the professional historians. Social scientists today accept the notion of the basic unity of the human mind. They recognize many cultural parallelisms and institutional stages in social evolution, even though these parallelisms and stages are not always inevitable or the sequences universal. These contributions are not only of permanent value and validity, but they form working hypotheses of all social scientists worthy of the name, even of those who ostensibly and formally repudiate the older evolutionism, root and branch.

---

1. Barnes and Becker, *op. cit.*, Chap. XIX.
2. H. E. Barnes *et al.*, *An Introduction to the History of Sociology* (Chicago: University of Chicago Press, 1947), Chap. VIII.
3. *Ibid.*, Chap. XIX.
4. *Ibid.*, Chap. XVI.
5. Keller, *op. cit.* (New York: Macmillan, 1915), pp. 114–115.
6. H. E. Barnes, Ed., *The History and Prospects of the Social Sciences* (New York: Knopf, 1925), Chap. V.
7. Herbert Spencer, *An Autobiography* (New York: Appleton, 1904, 2 vols.), Vol. II, pp. 324–326.
8. H. E. Barnes and Howard Becker, *Contemporary Social Theory* (New York: Appleton-Century, 1940), p. 442.
9. Barnes *et al.*, *op cit.*, Chap. V; and B. J. Stern, *Lewis Henry Morgan: Social Evolutionist* (Chicago: University of Chicago Press, 1931).
10. L. H. Morgan, *Ancient Society* (New York: Holt, 1877); cited in Stern, *op. cit.*, pp. 131–132.
11. White, in Barnes, *et al.*, *op. cit.*, Chap. V.
12. For a sympathetic and appreciative estimate of Frazer, see Bronislaw Malinowski, *A Scientific Theory of Culture* (Chapel Hill: University of North Carolina Press, 1944), pp. 179–221; for a critical estimate, see Lowie, *op. cit.*, pp. 101–104; and Alexander Goldenweiser, *History, Psychology and Culture* (New York: Knopf, 1933), pp. 167–178.

CHAPTER III

THE TRANSITION FROM EVOLUTIONARY ANTHROPOLOGY TO SCIENTIFIC AND CRITICAL STUDY OF SOCIAL ORIGINS

I. THE ROLE AND WORK OF SIR EDWARD BURNETT TYLOR

In the writings of several anthropologists and historical sociologists we may discover a gradual transition from uncritical evolutionism to scientific and inductive anthropology as illustrated by the works of Marett in England, Ehrenreich and others in Germany, and Boas and his followers in the United States.

Perhaps the first of these transitional figures was a scholar who is often inaccurately lumped with the early evolutionists, Sir Edward Burnett Tylor (1832–1917). His chief works were *Researches into the Early History of Mankind* (1865); and *Primitive Culture* (1871),[1] of which the latter is the more important and is one of the great anthropological classics. It was in this work that Tylor presented at length his famous theory of Animism as the primordial basis of religious thought and practice. Tylor epitomized his views on primitive life in his *Anthropology* (1881), which, after nearly seventy years, remains unexcelled as a mellow and judicious introduction to the subject.

Tylor accepted the evolutionary and comparative method, but he did so in a very discriminating fashion, and he foreshadowed many of the later and more critical attitudes and methods. Tylor's most important contribution to evolutionism was his doctrine of "survivals" in culture. He held that these vestiges from earlier periods of human experience can serve as a valid means of reconstructing the stages of cultural and social evolution. Tylor anticipated Westermarck by a generation in rejecting the idea of any unilateral evolution of the family from chaotic promiscuity to monogamy. While accepting the idea of independent development of institutions and cultural traits, he also fully recognized the existence and importance of cultural contacts and diffusion in the growth of human institutions. As early as 1889, he forecast the later proposals of Mazzarella, Steinmetz and Hobhouse to apply statistical methods to the study of the evolution of primitive social institutions. He also, along with Lippert, adumbrated A. L. Kroeber's notion that cultural evolution is "super-organic" and, hence, cannot be logically explained by biological methods. All in all, Tylor may be regarded as one of the founders of the idea that historical sociology is basically a science of cultural development which must be studied primarily by methods and laws peculiar to itself—what is now being called "culturology."

II. EDWARD ALEXANDER WESTERMARCK: FAIRLY SOUND RESULTS BY UNSOUND METHODS

Edward Alexander Westermarck (1862–1939), who was born about the time that Tylor published his first important book, is the best example of an evolutionary anthropologist and historical sociologist who arrived at the right ideas by using the uncritical comparative methods of the evolutionists.[2] It was Westermarck's aim to establish through sociology a natural history of institutions, based on Darwinian assumptions. He applied these ideas to the history of human marriage and to the nature and development of moral concepts and practices. In both cases, his fundamental ideas, while not always novel or unique, have been generally accepted as sound. Yet, in seeking confirmation and illustrations of his basic contentions, he followed much the same method as that outlined by Herbert Spencer. In short, most of his assertions as to the history of marriage and the origins of morals are accurate, but in respect to methodology he made little progress beyond Spencer and Morgan, and can hardly be regarded as being equal to Tylor in critical discrimination as to anthropological methodology and sources.

Westermarck's most famous work is his *History of Human Marriage,* which first appeared in 1891, and was subsequently enlarged and reprinted many times, reaching three volumes in the edition of 1921. Westermarck rejected the contention of the evolutionary anthropologists that the family has invariably evolved from primitive promiscuity to monogamy. He held that a paternal or patrilineal monogamy was the earliest and most usual form of marriage, from the first human societies to the present day. Other forms of the family have always been a special manifestation of institutional growth, to be explained by unusual conditions affecting family life in a given period or area. In cases where descent was traced through females, this had been preceded by paternal descent. His thesis of a predominant monogamy has now been generally accepted by anthropologists and historical sociologists. But when Westermarck sought to illustrate and confirm his fundamental doctrines regarding the family, he gathered vast masses of comparative materials by exactly the same slips-of-paper method which had been employed by Spencer and the early evolutionists. If there was any improvement in the illustrative material, it was primarily due to the fact that Westermarck lived and worked a generation later and had more and better sources to use rather than to any actual improvement in his theoretical methodology.

Westermarck's notions relative to the nature, sources and development of moral ideas were embodied in his *Origin and Development of the Moral Ideas* (1906–08), which appeared in expanded form in two volumes in 1917; in works on religion, marriage, and ceremonials in Morocco; and in a theoretical work, *Ethical Relativity* (1932). He sought to develop a natural, evolutionary theory of moral origins and development, buttressed by instinctivist psychology, and to demonstrate the secular origin and relativistic nature of moral conceptions and practices. In this he succeeded. But, once more, his illustrative materials were compiled and presented in the old evolutionary and comparative manner. The main advance over older writers in Westermarck's books lay in the fact that Westermarck had spent much time in actual field work and residence among the natives of Morocco. But when he went elsewhere in books for other ethnographic materials he still remained true to the comparative and evolutionary methods.

III. ROBERT BRIFFAULT AND THE RENAISSANCE OF MATRIARCHALISM

Nearly forty years after the first edition of Westermarck's *History of Human Marriage* appeared, its basic contentions were challenged by the most voluminous and impressive statement ever made of the case for an original and primordial matriarchal foundation of primitive society—a theory set forth by J. J. Bachofen nearly seventy years earlier. This was contained in Robert Briffault's *The Mothers* (3 vols., 1927).[3] Briffault did not contend that there had ever been any universal condition or stage of primitive society in which the women actually ruled or directly dominated those who did formally rule. What he did contend, on the basis of a vast amount of evidence assembled by the same comparative method which Westermarck used, was that, in primitive society, the rôle and influence of females (mothers) were vastly greater than that of the males in creating the social mind, group sentiments, and the social institutions of the race. Accepting John Fiske's idea of the importance of the prolongation of the period of infancy as a main factor in socializing mankind, Briffault contended that the particular duty and function of socializing the individual—imparting social education (group tradition)—fell upon the mothers in society: "The social characters of the human mind are, one and all, traceable to the operations of instincts that are related to the functions of the female and not to those of the male."

Whatever the validity or falsity of Briffault's attempt to rehabilitate a discriminating version of the matriarchal theory, so far as method in historical sociology is concerned, his book is important mainly as the most elaborate and voluminous revival of the comparative method since the heyday of the evolutionary anthropologists during the last third of the nineteenth century.

IV. JULIUS LIPPERT AND THE EVOLUTION OF CULTURE

Of all the Germanic anthropologists and historical sociologists who represented the transition from extreme evolutionism to critical cultural anthropology Julius Lippert (1839–1909) may well be regarded as the most productive and important.[4] In many ways he might be called the E. B. Tylor of Germany. Like Tylor, he accepted the comparative and evolutionary method in a discriminating and qualified manner. He held that culture is superorganic and not directly subject to the laws of biological determinism. Also, he resembled Tylor in calling attention to the importance of the diffusion as well as the independent development of institutions and cultural traits, and in giving special attention to religious elements in culture.

But Lippert far surpassed Tylor in the production of books. Whereas Tylor wrote only one great classic, his *Primitive Culture,* Lippert produced more than a half-dozen substantial books on the evolution of institutions, cultural development and social history. In the field of religious development, Lippert's chief works were: *Der Seelencult* (1880); *Die Religionen der europäischen Culturvölker* (1881); *Christenthum, Volksglaube und Volksbrauch* (1882); and *Allgemeine Geschichte der Priesterthums* (1884). He also wrote a comprehensive history of the family, *Die Geschichte der Familie* (1884). On the basis of these and other researches into cultural and institutional history, he produced an introduction to cultural history in his *Die Kulturgeschichte in einzelnen Hauptstücken* (1886), which he later expanded into his classic work, *Die Kulturgeschichte der Menschheit in ihrem organischen Aufbau* (1887), the more important portions of which have been translated into English by Professor George P. Murdock as *The Evolution of Culture* (1931). Lippert had originally been interested in history, and in 1889 he published an important work on German social history, *Deutsche Sittengeschichte;* and in 1898 he brought out what is regarded as his most scholarly work, a social history of early Bohemia, *Social-Geschichte Böhmens in vorhussitischer Zeit.* His interest and competence in both comparative anthropology and social history suggest a comparison with the Russian scholar, Maksim Kovalesky, whose work we shall discuss later on.

While Lippert accepted the general conceptions of evolutionary and comparative anthropology and such items as the reality and sequence of maternal and paternal society, he did so in a discriminating fashion. He adopted a broad approach to cultural evolution, and upheld the doctrine of the organic unity of cultural growth and the idea of the continuity of cultural and institutional development. But he recognized that evolutionary processes are not always progressive, rejected the idea of inevitable unilateral evolution and parallel cultural development, and maintained that there are no universal patterns of institutional and cultural growth or invariable stages of institutional evolution. We have already indicated that he agreed with Tylor in stressing the diffusion of cultural traits, as well as their independent development, and in holding that cultural evolution is a superorganic process to be studied by cultural anthropology and history rather than social biology. In his emphasis on the primacy of economic factors in the growth of culture and institutions Lippert resembled Morgan.

Lippert's influence was most marked on German anthropology and social and cultural history. He had only a slight following in England, where the comparable notions of Tylor held sway. In the United States, Lippert was mainly esteemed by William Graham Sumner and Albert G. Keller. His influence was marked on Sumner's *Folkways* and on the Sumner-Keller *Science of Society*. Indeed, his influence and materials were as dominant in Sumner's anthropology and comparative sociology as were the notions of Spencer in Sumner's political philosophy and sociological individualism.

V. FRANZ MÜLLER-LYER AND ALFRED VIERKANDT: HISTORICAL SOCIOLOGY AS A SCIENCE OF CULTURAL EVOLUTION

One of the most important of German historical sociologists, so far as the production of books on social evolution is concerned, was Franz Carl Müller-Lyer (1857–1916).[5] He has been called by some the "German Letourneau" because of the number of books he wrote which rigorously adhered to the evolutionary formula. But he was well trained as a psychiatrist, as well as a sociologist, and he had much keener insight and more discriminating judgment than Letourneau. Moreover, his sociological writings appeared a generation after those of Letourneau, so he was able to use better materials and more critical methods. Müller-Lyer defined culture as "the sum of all man's progress and achievements and their resulting manners and customs."

Sociology he regarded as the science of the analysis and evolution of culture.

Müller-Lyer combined the Spencerian evolutionary dogmas, unilateral evolutionary anthropological conceptions, and economic determinism. But he repudiated Spencerian individualism and, like Oppenheimer, was chiefly interested in social evolution as a means of illuminating and supporting a reformist program. Whereas Oppenheimer looked to agrarian producers' coöperatives for the solution of our economic crisis, Müller-Lyer relied upon labor organizations, or workers' associations, to bring about economic and social justice.

He maintained that there are universal laws of social evolution which apply among all peoples. These are, chiefly, the Spencerian laws that social development moves from the simple to the complex, and from the homogeneous to the heterogeneous. These laws of social evolution give rise to universal and invariable stages of social and cultural development. There may be no exact and complete duplication of trends and stages of social development among all the peoples of the world, but there is such duplication in all essentials, and the variations are much less important, numerous and noticeable than the identities. Moreover, it is necessary to establish the identities before the local differences can be fruitfully studied.

In his conception of social dynamics, Müller-Lyer adhered to the doctrine of economic determinism. Economic factors are dominant in society and culture. Each new cultural epoch is brought into being by improvements in technology and the application of labor to production. Like Vierkandt, Müller-Lyer anticipated Ogburn by years in his idea of cultural lag. He showed that cultural traits and institutions vary in the rate of their evolution. Especially do social institutions fail to keep pace with scientific and technological advances in modern times. The present economic and social crisis is due to the failure to provide for adequate mass purchasing power on the part of workers and farmers. Through the pressure of workers' associations we may create an economy which will bring consumption into adjustment with production. This will in time produce a socialist economy, but we may expect state socialism ultimately to give way to a coöperative workers' commonwealth in which the functions of the state will be reduced to a minimum.

Müller-Lyer entitled his general project of social evolution, *The Evolutionary Stages of Mankind* (*Entwicklungsstufen der Menschheit*), and he produced seven volumes in this series, covering such subjects as the evolution of knowledge, love, marriage, the family, material culture, and education; and a study of heredity. The best outline of his evolutionary scheme is contained in his *Phasen der Kultur und Richtungslinien der Fortschritts* (1908), which was translated into English in 1920 under the title of *The History of Social Development*. While his methods savored a good deal of the older evolutionism, few historical sociologists have assembled more varied and important materials or presented them in more lucid fashion.

In the generation following Lippert's main work, another German historical sociologist, Alfred Vierkandt (1867–   ), set forth an even more extreme doctrine of cultural determinism in his *Naturvölker und Kulturvölker* (1896); and his *Die Stetigkeit im Kulturwandel* (1908).[6] Vierkandt upheld the conception of absolute cultural determinism in the evolution of culture and institutions and stressed the notion of cultural continuity. He believed that cultural and institutional development must be studied by means of a science of culture, and in this stage of his scholarly work he held that sociology should be primarily a theory of cultural evolution.

It was Vierkandt's idea that there is little that is spontaneous or a matter of chance in cultural growth and institutional development. Culture and institutions are the product of the past accumulation of items and trends, and their nature and growth are always determined by the background of any social group. There can be few new developments which are not in accord with the conditions prepared by past group experience. The "great man" is unimportant in cultural history. When cultural conditions are favorable, inventions and growth will take place, and there will be many parallel and comparable inventions when the cultural background is similar. Vierkandt completely rejected the idea of the evolutionary anthropologists that there are universal and unilateral cultural trends and stages of development. Even the diffusion of culture is unlikely or difficult unless a given group is prepared to receive the cultural traits passed along by contacts with other groups. He clearly understood the fact of "cultural lag," or the failure of certain institutions to develop at the same rate as others and the inability of institutions as a whole to keep pace with technological evolution. His ideas of cultural determinism were in general accord with those of Clark Wissler, and he anticipated by more than a decade William F. Ogburn's doctrine of "cultural lag."

VI. MAKSIM KOVALEVSKY: RUSSIAN SOCIAL EVOLUTIONIST AND INSTITUTIONAL HISTORIAN

Of all the historical sociologists of the past generation probably the most accurate scholar, the most capable generalizer, and the most prolific author was the Russian, Maksim Maksimovich Kovalevsky (1851–1916).[7] Like Lippert, Kovalevsky was both a cultural anthropologist and a social historian. Like Westermarck, he spent considerable time in the field studying primitive culture and cultural survivals, visiting the Caucasus as Westermarck had Morocco. In addition, he was a well-trained technical historian in the handling of documentary and archival materials. He ranged over a vast area of subjects, from technical works on late medieval English and Continental institutional history to comparative studies of such institutions as government, law, the family, and property. He was influenced especially by Comte, Spencer, Sir Henry Sumner Maine, and the evolutionary anthropologists who dominated the situation during his youth. From Comte he took over the Positivist method and the idea of the interdependence of social factors. From Spencer he derived the idea of universal evolution and his theory of automatic and inevitable progress. From Maine he secured inspiration in the comparative and historical study of institutions, and from the evolutionary anthropologists he accepted the idea of cultural and institutional evolution.

Kovalevsky's first important writings were devoted to the social and economic history of England and western Europe at the close of the Middle Ages. Then, he wrote important books on comparative legal and institutional history. Next, he brought out several books on the economic and political development of Russia and on the economic and social history of France from the Middle Ages to the Revolution. One of his most famous works was his *Economic History of Europe to the Rise of Capitalism* (7 vols. 1901–1915), in which he stressed the importance of growing density of population for economic development. He also produced voluminous treatises on the origins of modern democracy and the rise of representative government. In 1910, Kovalevsky brought out two volumes of his *Sociology,* of which several other volumes were to follow, but his work was disrupted by the outbreak of war in 1914 and he died in broken health in 1916.

His work in social and economic history was characterized by great erudition, brilliant scholarship, and unusual powers of synthesis and generalization. As a cultural anthropologist and historical sociologist his writings were dominated by a life-long effort to adjust the unilateral evolutionism of his youthful period to his awareness of the progress in anthropological methods during his lifetime. Evolutionism and the comparative method provided the framework of his thought and writings, but he tried to temper this with knowledge of the newer and more critical trends.

The older evolutionism expressed itself in many ways in his books. He held that the basic law of sociology is that of universal progress. He said that we can observe many cultural and institutional similarities in societies that are widely dispersed in space and could not possibly have had contacts or consciously imitated each other. He believed in the reality of identical stages of cultural and institutional development among such peoples. This, he said, could only be explained on the basis of the fundamental unity of history.

In his "Genetic Sociology," which constituted the second volume of his *Sociology,* Kovalevsky set forth his conception of the desirable method in historical sociology. This consists in working out the stages of social evolution and then formulating the laws which govern the development and sequence of these stages. He held that the primary task of historical sociology is to establish the similarities in cultural and institutional evolution. He maintained that we can discern many instances of a transition from matrilineal to patrilineal descent, but can find no examples of the reverse trend. He worked out his own panorama of the stages in social evolution, which were: (1) the horde, when the matrilineal family dominated; (2) the gens in which the patrilineal family was predominant; (3) patriarchal nomadism; (4) feudalism; and (5) democracy.

Symptoms of his awareness of the qualifications enforced upon the older evolutionism by newer methods and data were the following: he held that social evolution is something quite different from biological evolution and that social development does not follow the laws of organic growth. The organismic theory of society cannot explain social evolution. In using the comparative method, examples of cultural conditions and alleged evidences of institutional parallelisms must not be torn from their context in the total cultural complex of the group. The totality of group culture must always be taken into consideration. Comparisons must be truly comparable in relation to the total cultural context and must represent comparable stages and types of cultural development. He thus repudiated the slips-of-paper method of compilation used by Spencer and Westermarck. He emphasized the dangers of universalism in generalization as to social evolution, making special use of the subject of totemism to illustrate this point. He laid stress upon the necessity of studying variations as well as identities in social evolution. From Comte's notion of the interdependence of factors he derived his own emphasis on the pluralistic nature of social causation. There was, thus, always a kind of dualism in Kovalevsky's historical sociology—a hangover of his earlier evolutionism along with acceptance of later critical qualifications. The former element was dominant and the opposing or qualifying views were never fully integrated into a coherent system.

VII. TRANSITIONAL TRENDS IN THE UNITED STATES

In the United States, the transition from the older comparative method to critical anthropology has been best exhibited by the works of William Graham Sumner, George Elliott Howard, Hutton Webster and William I. Thomas. Sumner (1840–1910) and his disciple, Keller, were influenced more by Lippert than by any other of the comparative anthropologists.[8] Sumner's most famous work was his *Folkways* (1907), a monumental and stimulating study of the origin and nature of customs, morals and social attitudes. More comprehensive was the *Science of Society* in four volumes (1927–1928), completed by Keller from Sumner's manuscript and notes. It was ably digested by Keller in his *Man's Rough Road* (1932), and redigested in his *Brass Tacks* (1938).

With the exception of Morgan, the most notable of the American contributions to social evolutionism was contained in the work of George Elliott Howard (1849–1928) on *The History of Matrimonial Institutions,* which appeared in three volumes in 1904. Howard had been trained as an institutional historian under the influence of the Germanic school of historians and its adaptation by Herbert Baxter Adams at Johns Hopkins University. His *Introduction to the Local Constitutional History of the United States* (1889) was an important book exemplifying the then popular effort to derive Anglo-American institutions from their alleged Germanic background and sources. His *History of Matrimonial Institutions* was a monumental effort to trace the origins and evolution of the family on the basis of comparative and evolutionary anthropology. He was influenced by Westermarck as well as by the earlier evolutionists, and it would not be unfair to regard Howard as the American Westermarck.[9]

Hutton Webster (1875–   ) was, like Lippert and Kovalevsky, an anthropologist and a talented professional historian. His three chief works in cultural anthropology were monographs which followed the comparative method in discriminating fashion. The first, *Primitive Secret Societies* (1908), subtitled "A Study in Early Politics and Religion," was a description of the important primitive societies that cut across clan lines and helped on the transition to civil society—an important phase of anthropological analysis which had been developed a few years earlier in Germany by Heinrich Schurtz. The second was *Rest Days* (1916), subtitled "A Study in Early Law and Morality," and devoted primarily to an account of days on which work and other normal activities were tabooed. The third was an important study of primitive "thou-shalt-nots," entitled *Taboo: A Sociological Study* (1942). Webster's critical sense and his training as an historian saved him from the more serious pitfalls in using the comparative method.

William Isaac Thomas (1863–1947) exhibited more interest in primitive culture than any other American sociologist of his generation, except for Sumner, Keller and Webster.[10] His first work was the masterly *Source Book for Social Origins* (1909), which was designed to illustrate important socio-psychological principles, such as control, habit, attention and crises, from carefully selected anthropological sources. Nearly thirty years later, he replaced this work by his book on *Primitive Behavior* (1937) in which the amount of interpretative textual material was relatively greatly increased and the cultural mode of analysis gained at the expense of the socio-psychological. Since Thomas was a careful and lifelong student of anthropological literature, always had a skeptical attitude towards grandiose generalization, and was acquainted in detail with the progress of anthropological thought, his works give little cause for criticism in regard to methodology. They make little pretense, however, to tracing social evolution beyond primitive forms of thought and behavior, though, of course, the majority of Thomas' other books deal with contemporary society.

---

1. Lowie, *op. cit.,* Chap. VII.
2. Barnes *et al., op. cit.,* Chap. XXXIII.
3. *Ibid.,* Chap. XXXIV.
4. G. P. Murdock, Introduction to his translation of Lippert's *The Evolution of Culture* (New York: Macmillan, 1931).
5. Article by Gottfried Salomon on Müller-Lyer, in *Encyclopaedia of the Social Sciences,* XI, pp. 83–84.
6. Theodore Abel, *Systematic Sociology in Germany* (New York: Columbia University Press, 1929), Chap. II.
7. Barnes *et al., op cit.,* Chap. XXIII.
8. *Ibid.,* Chap. VI.
9. See articles on Howard in *Sociology and Social Research,* XIII (1928–1929), pp. 11–17, 108–118, 229–233.
10. Barnes *et al., op. cit.,* Chap. XL.

CHAPTER IV

THE TRIUMPH OF SCIENTIFIC METHOD IN HISTORICAL SOCIOLOGY *

I. ÉMILE DURKHEIM'S REVOLT: INTENSIVE STUDY OF A SINGLE CULTURE AREA VERSUS THE COMPARATIVE METHOD

The first sociologist of note thoroughly to reject the comparative method in a published work of significance was the leader of French sociology, Émile Durkheim (1858–1917).[1] In his *Les Formes élémentaires de la vie religieuse* (1912), he rejected the procedure of the comparative school in attempting to derive the laws of social evolution from the study of many social institutions as they have appeared in most diverse regions and periods of time. He contended that any valid conclusions as to social evolution must rest rather upon an intensive study of a single social institution on the basis of its manifestations in one definite cultural area. For his own work he selected the development of religion, especially totemism, in Australia.

Critics have insisted, however, that Durkheim went to the other extreme from the procedure followed by the comparative school and introduced almost as many methodological errors as he had rejected. No intensive study of a single institution in one cultural area can establish any law of institutional or cultural growth. Only a discriminating comparison and analysis of carefully gathered and critically sifted data from many cultural areas can accomplish this result. Further, Australian ethnography and ethnology had not been pursued with sufficient critical care to make the available data of sufficient reliability to justify dogmatic generalizations even for that continent alone. As Alexander Goldenweiser has well said of this aspect of Durkheim's work: "The fact itself that the author felt justified in selecting the Australian area for his intensive analysis shows plainly enough how far from realization still is the goal which his own life-work has at least made feasible, the rapprochement of ethnology and sociology."

It seems to be agreed that, as a basis for sociological generalization, Durkheim's intensive study of primitive religion is almost as unreliable as the results of Frazer's studies pursued by the unrestrained comparative method. The value of his book must be found in the author's sociological and psychological acumen and not in the reliability of the method of investigation or of the ethnographic material adduced to substantiate the conclusions. Durkheim's outstanding contribution in this field was his emphatic demonstration of the social origins and basis of religion and ceremonial life.

II. BRONISLAW MALINOWSKI AND MARGARET MEAD

A methodological approach resembling that of Durkheim— the one-man study of a special area or cultural trait—was that of the Polish anthropologist, Bronislaw Malinowski (1884– 1942).[2] He made a number of interesting studies of primitive life, especially law and sex, among the natives of the Pacific islands. Some of his more important books were *The Family among the Australian Aborigines* (1913) ; *The Natives of Mailu* (1915) ; *Argonauts of the Western Pacific* (1922) ; *Crime and Custom in Savage Society* (1926) ; *The Father in Primitive Psychology* (1927) ; *Sex and Repression in Savage Society* (1927) ; *The Sexual Life of Savages in Northwest Melanesia* (1929) ; and his main theoretical work, *A Scientific Theory of Culture* published posthumously in 1944. While Malinowski repudiated the universalism and unilateral evolutionism of the classical anthropologists, he was nearly as prone to sweeping generalizations, which were based on rather limited, if intensive, field studies. But he at least had extensive and prolonged contact with primitive peoples in their own habitat and did not formulate his doctrines from library research. Few anthropologists have written with greater fertility of imagination or more brilliant insight.

Another example of generalizing from studies of a special social factor in a particular area is Margaret Mead's work on sex and adolescence in Polynesia. On the basis of this she has generalized boldly not only on sex problems in all types of societies but even on current political and international problems. From *Growing Up in New Guinea* she has moved easily and confidently on to contemporary world policy in her *And Keep Your Powder Dry,* and to passing pontifical judgment upon the mentality of the German people.

III. LEONARD T. HOBHOUSE AND THE STATISTICAL APPROACH TO PRIMITIVE INSTITUTIONS

One of the most interesting innovations in method which has been the work of a historical sociologist was the attempt of Professor Leonard T. Hobhouse (1864–1929) to introduce the method of statistical correlation into the investigation of the evolution of primitive social institutions in their relation to the progress of material culture. In an earlier work, *Morals in Evolution,* Hobhouse had relied upon a critical utilization of the comparative method. Here he had contended that there were three main stages in the evolution of political society, in which the dominant principle has been successively: (1) kinship; (2) authority; and (3) citizenship. This excursus may, indeed, have impressed upon him the risks of this method.

In his *Material Culture and Social Institutions of the Simpler Peoples,*[3] Hobhouse proposed to introduce a new method of investigation through the statistical correlation of the stages in the progress of government and justice, the forms of the family, and the nature of war and its reaction upon social structure with the main epochs in the development of material culture. This was, in fact, as Hobhouse frankly admits, but an elaboration of the method proposed by Sir Edward Burnett Tylor in 1889 in his famous essay "On a Method of Investigating the Development of Institutions: Applied to the Laws of Marriage and Descent."[4] J. Mazzarella in his *Les Types sociaux et le droit* (1908) had also used the method of correlation in his effort to explain exogamy and various forms of primitive marriage on the basis of the theory of underpopulation.

Hobhouse offers the following excellent criticism of the comparative method and indicates the difficulty of establishing valid generalizations concerning social evolution:

Theories of social evolution are readily formed with the aid of some preconceived ideas and a few judiciously selected corroborative facts. The data offered to the theorist by the voluminous results of anthropological inquiry on the one hand, and by the immense record of the history of civilization on the other, are so vast and so various that it must be an unskilled selector who is unable, by giving prominence to the instances which agree and by ignoring those which conflict with his views, to make out a plausible case in support of some general notion of human progress. On the other hand, if theories are easily made, they are also easily confuted by a less friendly use of the same data. That same variety of which we speak is so great that there is hardly any sociological generalization which does not stumble upon some awkward fact if one takes the trouble to find it. Anyone with a sense for facts soon recognizes that the course of social evolution is not unitary but that different races and different communities of the same race have, in fact, whether they started from the same point or no, diverged early, rapidly, and in many different directions at once. If theorizing is easy when facts are treated arbitrarily, a theory which would really grow out of the facts themselves and express their true significance presents the greatest possible difficulties to the inquirer. The data themselves are vast but chaotic, and at every point incomplete. They fall into two main divisions. On the one hand, there is the historical record of the civilizations; upon the other there is the immense field of contemporary anthropology. In both alike the data are equally difficult to ascertain with precision, and when ascertained to reduce to any intelligible order. In the history of civilization we have full studies of many institutions, and we can learn something, not only of what they were at any one moment, but of their development in time, their genesis, their rise, their maturity, their decay. But even here the information often breaks off short at the most interesting point. Beginnings are frequently matter of conjecture. The nature of institutions, as they appear on paper, may be known to us, while we are left to reconstruct their actual working from causal examples, hints, and references that leave much to the imagination. We find them decaying without intelligible cause, and often enough we are faced with the fact that more thoroughgoing inquiry has completely revolutionized our view of an institution which had been taken as thoroughly explored and fully interpreted by earlier schools of historians. So is it also with anthropological record. Here indeed we have a handful of monographs made by trained and skilled observers in modern times, which leave nothing to be desired excepting that the work had been carried out three or four generations ago before contact with the white man or with other more civilized races had begun to corrupt the purity of aboriginal institutions. Outside these monographs we have a vast mass of traveller's reports, good, bad, and indifferent, data which it is impossible to ignore and yet which can seldom be taken at their face value. Moreover all anthropological data of this kind, however simple the life of the people with which they deal, are modern: with the exception of the few available references that we have to the peoples that surrounded the Greeks and Romans in Herodotus, Tacitus, and other writers of antiquity, the great bulk of anthropological inquiry dates from the last three or four centuries, and it is sometimes forgotten that the peoples of whom they treat must have lived as long, must in a sense have had as extensive a tradition behind them, and to that extent are as far removed from the true primitive as civilized man himself.[5]

Instead of using the comparative, descriptive and illustrative method of the older evolutionary school, Hobhouse and his associates, G. C. Wheeler and Morris Ginsberg, sought to discover whether there is any correlation between material culture, namely the arts of life, and certain leading social institutions—sex mores, marriage, family, government, war, etc. The authors first classified nearly all the primitive peoples recorded and described in anthropological reports and monographs and arranged them on the basis of their reported economic status and development. They then classified them, according to material development, in the following sequence: lower hunters, higher hunters, lower pastoral peoples, higher pastoral peoples, lowest agricultural peoples, higher agricultural peoples, and highest agricultural peoples (among primitive types). Thereupon, they sought to discover to what extent there is a correlation between (1) the development and complexity of the forms of government and law, the evolution of the family, and the prevalance, nature and results of war, and (2) the advances in material culture as reflected in the above progressive classification of primitive peoples.

The results were about what any trained and critical anthropologist or sociologist would have anticipated. There is some broad and general correlation between high material culture and the development and complexity of social institutions, but such correlation is neither close nor uniform. As would be expected, Hobhouse discovered that there is a fairly close correlation between high material culture and the existence of a relatively complex and powerful government. But it is also clear that there is no uniformity which would indicate that the details or forms of government conform to or keep pace with economic development in any precise way. Likewise, it was shown, as would have been anticipated, that organized warfare increases with the development of material culture which makes wars more worth fighting and provides better sinews of war. When we come to sex mores, marriage and the family, the correlation between these customs and institutions and material culture was shown to be even more loose and general, thus tending to upset the dogma of the evolutionists that marriage and the family developed in uniform and unilateral fashion from promiscuity to organized and deliberate monogamy, keeping step in each stage of development with parallel advances in material culture.

Critics have, naturally, called attention to certain serious defects in the execution of Hobhouse's project, while admitting the value of the method if the data were adequate and the detailed application rigid. They have alleged that, by his arbitrary division of primitive peoples into the lower and higher hunters, etc., Hobhouse inevitably obtained from his study what he had assumed at the outset in his preliminary classification. Again, his selection of the "tribe" as the statistical unit makes specific accuracy and definiteness impossible, because of the great variations in the nature of the tribe. To the author of this volume it seems that the most damaging criticism which may be directed against the work is Hobhouse's admission that the anthropological data gathered by skilled and critical investigators are not sufficient to warrant the undertaking of any such enterprise as he has attempted, and his subsequent willingness to use the highly unreliable material gathered by missionaries and travelers in the absence of trustworthy information. Further, a survey of the authorities used indicates that, like Durkheim, Hobhouse had not realized the serious methodological errors that had been involved in the procedure of compiling the material for such widely used monographs as Spencer and Gillen's monographs on the Australian data. In other words, not only did he fail to limit himself to reliable anthropological monographs, but he also failed to discriminate critically between the relative reliability of the monographs used. Having brilliantly described the unreliable, incomplete and confused character of many anthropological works, he then proceeded to use some of this very material as the basis of his excursion into quantitative ethnology.

Even before Hobhouse set forth his advocacy of the use of statistics in anthropology and the study of primitive culture, the Dutch sociologist, S. R. Steinmetz had also indicated the need for this method. He developed the idea of sociography or descriptive sociology, which describes and analyzes various social and cultural entities. His best statement of the rôle and tasks of sociography was contained in an article on "Die Stellung der Soziographie in der Reihe der Geisteswissenschaften" (1913). He contended that sociography must, if it is to be scientific in procedure, make wide use of statistical compilation and analysis.

IV. THE CULTURE CASE STUDY APPROACH TO HISTORICAL SOCIOLOGY

A fundamental tenet of the evolutionary and comparative school of anthropologists and historical sociologists was the assumption of the basic unity of the human mind, the universality of major cultural traits and institutions, and the similarity and invariable sequence of the stages of cultural and institutional development. The field and range of investigation were regarded as relatively unlimited as to time, space or theme, and the main aim in such studies was the ability to generalize at large as to social evolution.

The most complete opposition to this attitude is what we know as Historicism,[6] represented by some of the more extreme members of the Boas school of anthropologists, such as Paul Radin, by Wilhelm Windelband, Heinrich Rickert, and Karl Heussi, who held that history can only discover and portray the unique, and by Ernst Troeltsch, who contended that we can discover historical trends only in the case of particular and special cultures. The extreme Historicists either contend that there are no universal trends in evolution (Windelband-Rickert), or that, if they are, we have no means of discovering them (Radin and Troeltsch).

The more moderate Historicists maintain that, while there may be definite trends and stages in social evolution, we do not as yet have enough information to justify extensive generalizations. Most members of the so-called Boas school are usually regarded as moderate Historicists, but Boas himself, Wissler, Kroeber and Goldenweiser have been sympathetic towards restrained generalizations about cultural development.

A compromise between extreme evolutionism and extreme Historicism has been worked out in what has been called "the culture case study method." [7] This starts with a limited theme or topic in culture or social institutions, tests it out in a particular period and place, and then tries to discover how far and in how many cases the principles and trends established will apply in other times and areas. This method combines the zest for accuracy in the case studied, which has been manifested by the Boas school and the Historicists, with the interest which the evolutionists had in generalization. Durkheim's rebellion against extreme evolutionism, which we have already discussed, was a good example of culture case study; he limited himself to a study of religion among the primitive tribes of Australia. Max Weber (1864–1920), the eminent German sociologist, was one of the more notable exemplars of the culture case study method in his works on ancient agrarian societies, the interrelation of religion and capitalism in early modern European society and in the

Far East, and the growth of rationalism. Arnold J. Toynbee executed the most elaborate enterprise in culture case study in his *A Study of History* (1933–1939). Here he worked out a theory of social evolution from a case study of Greco-Roman civilization and then applied it to some twenty other historic civilizations from Korea to Yucatan. Unfortunately Toynbee's effort, as we shall see later on, was as extreme a variant from sound social science as the wildest evolutionary sallies of Letourneau or Frazer. The evolutionists accepted uncritically, as their fundamental article of faith, Darwinian or Spencerian naturalistic evolution. Toynbee substituted for that a refurbished Christian Epic and a theodicean spiritual interpretation of history. Then, after having formulated his "case" from a one-sided theological and spiritualized interpretation of Greco-Roman civilization, he applied his schematic interpretation to all the other historic civilizations as uncritically as any evolutionist ever utilized evolutionary dogmas and the stage pattern of social development.

A variant of the culture case study method which has much impressed sociologists is the formulation of what Max Weber called the Ideal-Typical procedure in historical sociology.[8] For the purpose of intensive study of a cultural situation, Weber proposed an ideal construct or type—an arbitrarily assumed form of personality reaction, social process, or social structure—that can be empirically established, isolated and then studied in detail. After this is done, the truths discovered about the cultural type or pattern studied can then be extended experimentally to other comparable times and places, in order to ascertain how far the original formulation holds true and to what extent it fails to conform to the facts in other situations. The Ideal-Typical assumption or situation is, thus no absolute dogma with definite value-judgments, but only a workable tool of empirical social and historical analysis, on the basis of which valid generalizations and causal relationships may possibly be established. In Weber's own excursions into culture case study and historical sociology the basic Ideal-Type for study and comparison was the growth of the rational habit of thought and the resulting secularization of society.

Weber's most famous application of the culture case study method was contained in his classic analysis of the relation between the ethical ideas of Protestantism and the rise of capitalistic principles and practices contained in his *Die protestantische Ethik und der Geist der Kapitalismus* (1905).[9] Having established the facts about the interrelation between religion, capitalism and rationality in western Europe in early modern times, he applied this Ideal-Typical case to the relation of religious ideas to economic life and habits of thought in India and China in his *Gesammelte Aufsätze zur Religionssoziologie* (1920), and found that the effects and relationships were almost the reverse of the situation he had discovered in the rise of European capitalism and the rational habit of mind. Weber's premature death brought to an untimely end what would probably have been the most important contribution made by any sociologist to the field of historical sociology.

V. HISTORICAL SOCIOLOGY AS AS EVOLUTIONARY SCIENCE OF CULTURE

We have already pointed out that Vierkandt regarded historical sociology as a science of cultural change, but he never developed this line of work systematically, having later turned his interests to phenomonology and abstraction. Durkheim also sought to work out a science of culture or culturology. But the most complete development of the idea that historical sociology is a science of culture was embodied in the work of Alfred Weber (1868–   ), the younger brother of Max Weber.[10] His best formulation of this conception is contained in his *Kultur-geschichte als Kultursoziologie* (1935).

Weber was trained in history, especially cultural and economic history, under Karl Lamprecht and Gustav Schmoller. He maintained that sociology must be regarded as a cultural rather than a natural science. Like Max Weber, he sought a methodological course and principle midway between the extreme Historicism, which denies any continuity or universality in historical development, and uncritical evolutionism. To forward this aim he divided the totality of the historical experience of mankind into three spheres or processes: (1) the social process; (2) the civilizational process; and (3) the cultural process.

The social process embodies the historical development of national and imperial societies from antiquity to the present time. Weber holds that there is here to be found no evidence of continuous and universal development which will permit broad generalizations as to sequence and stages of growth. There are, however, many instances of interrelationship and interdependence. But the only accurate and satisfactory method of studying the social process consists in the use of the Ideal-Typical method, by which such similarities and generalizations as exist may be empirically established and the variations noted.

The civilizational process relates to the material development of humanity—the conquest of physical nature by mankind. Here there is plenty of evidence of continuous progress and the handing along of achievements. Broad generalizations as to inventions, diffusion, accumulation and transitions are here permissible and fruitful.

The cultural process, which covers the arts and things of the spirit, constitutes the realm of the unique in human experience. Culture, in this sense, is creative and spontaneous. There is no demonstrable progress in this field, and no universal laws of development or growth exist.

Interesting and suggestive as Weber's views may be, much the same ideas of progress in these three fields or processes of human experience had been set forth by Bernard de Fontenelle in his *Digression on the Ancients and the Moderns* away back in 1688.

VI. THE RISE OF CRITICAL CULTURAL ANTHROPOLOGY: THE BOAS SCHOOL

We have noted that, in the writings of such anthropologists and historical sociologists as Tylor, Lippert, Kovalevsky, Vierkandt, and others, many qualifications and doubts were raised as to the complete validity of the older unilateral evolutionism of earlier writers like Spencer and Morgan. But the thorough repudiation of such methods and the establishment of scientific and critical, or historico-analytical, anthropology have been chiefly associated with the work of Franz Boas, an eminent American anthropologist, and his followers, such as Clark Wissler, A. L. Kroeber, Robert H. Lowie, Alexander Goldenweiser, Edward Sapir, Fay-Cooper Cole, Ruth Benedict, Paul Radin, and others. Marett espoused similar ideas in England, albeit less rigorously, as also did Vierkandt, Ehrenreich and Thurnwald in Germany.[11] Boas had received a rigorous scientific training as a physicist and anthropogeographer in Germany and he applied these critical scientific methods to the study of primitive culture and institutions.

Boas and his associates rejected those phases of the older evolutionary anthropology which were based upon organismic theories of society, upon biological and social analogies, and upon the comparative school's idea of the universal and inevitable unilateral evolution of culture and institutions, following much the same pattern the world over. They took up and developed the suggestions of Tylor and Lippert that culture, including social institutions, is a super-organic matter, an idea most explicitly stated by Kroeber. Hence, cultural evolution cannot be founded on biological evolution. It presents a different field of phenomena and requires different methods. There is no inherent logic in the assumption that cultural evolution exhibits any of the laws or trends of biological evolution. The only connection between biology and cultural anthropology is a mutual adherence to the methodology which must dominate all science, biological or cultural, namely, the contention that an empirical study of data must precede the formulation of any scientific laws.

Hence, the Boas school has insisted upon the necessity of a thorough study of culture in the field among primitive peoples before attempting to formulate any sweeping laws of cultural evolution. They thus completely repudiate the slips-of-paper method of anthropological research and generalization as practiced from Spencer to Westermarck. They assert that the unit of investigation should be what they call a *culture area,* or a geographical region where the culture and institutions of the primitive inhabitants are a relatively similar and a unified, though not necessarily, unique complex. They hold that not enough research of a reliable sort has yet been done in specific culture areas to permit grandiose schemes of generalization, though enough has been accomplished to disprove the validity of much earlier generalization of this type. Some members of the school, like Paul Radin, in his *The Method and Theory of Ethnology* (1933) come pretty close to extreme Historicism and contend that each cultural area is essentially unique and not duplicated elsewhere, and, hence, that generalizations as to cultural evolution are not likely to be possible or valid. Others, such as Wissler, Goldenweiser and Kroeber—and even Boas himself— do not repudiate the possibility or desirability of generalization. They hold that one main purpose of intensive field work is to provide the empirical basis for anthropological generalization, just as empirical research in other fields of science is carried on primarily to permit the ultimate formulation of scientific laws. They only sound a note of caution about generalizing in advance of adequate research and valid data.

An eclectic and empirical attitude towards cultural development is also taken by the Harvard anthropologist, A. M. Tozzer, and by his colleague, Ronald B. Dixon, in his *The Building of Cultures* (1928), though Dixon's opinions were formulated quite independently of the Boas school. At Yale, George P. Murdock has espoused the principles of critical cultural anthropology. The Boas school has been vigorously criticized by Leslie A. White for its alleged adherence to the negative attitude of the extreme Historicists. White has sought to rehabilitate the evolutionism of Morgan, qualified and disciplined by further knowledge and more critical methods.

Whatever the paucity of the contributions of the Boas group to generalizations about cultural parallelisms, repetitions and evolution, they have rendered an important service in calling a halt to the older uncritical evolutionism, to the slips-of-paper fallacy, and to the lack of scientific procedure involved in generalizing prior to adequate research and accumulated materials.

VII. LESLIE A. WHITE AND CULTUROLOGY

Though the Boas school and other critical anthropologists held that the study of human society and institutions is a cultural rather than a biological problem, most of them, with the exception of Kroeber, have contended that culture must be interpreted in psychological or socio-psychological terms. They refused to concede the existence of a science of culture, independent of psychological laws and processes. The most ambitious and far-reaching attempt to establish the reality of a science of culture, or culturology, which must be handled in terms of cultural laws and processes alone, has been set forth by Leslie A. White in his article on "The Expansion of the Scope of Science" (1947). He summarizes his argument as follows:

The culturologist knows full well that cultural traits do not go walking about like disembodied souls interacting with each other. But he realizes that he can explain cultural phenomena as *cultural phenomena* only when he treats them *as if* they had a life of their own, quite apart from the glands, nerves, muscles, etc., of human organisms. . . .
It is not "we" who control our culture but our culture controls us. And our culture grows and changes according to its own laws. . . . It now remains to discover the principles of a million years of culture growth and to formulate the laws of this development.[12]

The main efforts of the critical anthropologists to work out laws of cultural development, thus far, have been related chiefly to the analysis of the principles of invention and independent development versus imitation and diffusion, or to suggest a discriminating synthesis of these opposing views. This controversy will be described briefly later on.

VIII. THE IMPACT OF CULTURAL ANTHROPOLOGY UPON AMERICAN SOCIOLOGY

Since critical cultural anthropolgy has been developed chiefly in the United States it was more or less natural that its first important impact upon historical sociology would be found in the United States. But its influence came slowly. Most American sociologists long accepted the evolutionary idea of the independent origins of culture and institutions and of their parallel development. The critical and analytical attitude was first evident to some degree in W. I. Thomas' *Source Book for Social Origins* (1909), for Thomas was an empirical and sceptical student of primitive society. He arrived at his critical ideas independently, though in later years he was directly affected by Boas and his school, as is evident in his *Primitive Behavior* (1937). One of the first comprehensive expositions of the views of the cultural anthropologists by a sociologist came from Charles Abram Ellwood in an article on "Theories of Cultural Evolution" (1918). Ellwood developed his interest in cultural anthropology as a result of his studies under Marett in 1914–1915. He soon became acquainted with the views of Boas and his school. Ellwood embodied his full exposition of the cultural approach in his book on *Cultural Evolution* (1927). More directly influenced by Boas was William Fielding Ogburn and his students, such as Malcolm M. Willey and Melville J. Herskovits. Ogburn developed his ideas of cultural evolution, emphasizing the notion of cultural lag, in his *Social Change* (1922). In an important article on "The Cultural Approach to Sociology" (1923), Willey and Herskovits set forth clearly the implications of this method for historical and analytical sociology. Herskovits, also a student of Boas, has developed his ideas more thoroughly in his book *Acculturation* (1938), a comprehensive study of the effects of cultural contacts between peoples. The cultural approach to sociology has now become rather generally accepted by the present generation of American sociologists, and is embodied in such systematic treatises as F. Stuart Chapin's *Cultural Change* (1928); Joseph K. Folsom's *Culture and Social Progress* (1928); and Wilson D. Wallis' *Culture and Progress* (1930).

Perhaps the most thoroughgoing development of the cultural type of analysis of historical and sociological material is contained in the work of Florian Znaniecki, collaborator with W. I. Thomas in their famous work on *The Polish Peasant in Europe and America* (1918–20). Znaniecki's main book on cultural sociology is his *Cultural Reality* (1919), which is an "attempt to state reality in terms of cultural interpretation." Unity can be given to the chaotic materials of social history by theoretically dividing them into four systems of reality—the physical order, the psychological order, the sociological order, and the ideal order. The physical order deals with the physical and biological aspects of human development. The psychological order handles the subjective phases of individual experience. The sociological order explains the relation between the various forms and areas of individual experience. The ideal order provides for the unification of social facts in an organized system of knowledge. As a whole, the book is a powerful argument for historical and cultural relativism.

IX. HISTORICAL SOCIOLOGY AND SOCIAL HISTORY IN THE UNITED STATES

While most sociologists in the United States today take heed of the cultural approach to social organization and problems, there have been few important systematic contributions to historical sociology in this country, and there has not been even one monumental book covering the whole period of human social evolution. The first great American contribution to historical sociology was Morgan's *Ancient Society,* which we have already described. No other book of equal sweep and influence has been produced. Giddings sketched the evolution of human society in masterly fashion in Book III of his *Principles of Sociology,* as we have already pointed out, but this was little more than the prospectus for a future work which Giddings never produced.

The American work on social evolution which probably ranks next to Morgan's book for its effect on American thought in the field of historical sociology was Brooks Adams' *Law of Civilization and Decay,* first published in 1895.[13] Adams sought to present the history of society as the human manifestation of dynamic, cosmic energy. As we shall discuss his theories in detail later on, we shall not deal with them in this place. The next important American contribution to historical sociology was embodied in Ernest W. Burgess' book, *The Function of Socialization in Social Evolution* (1916). Part II of this work was devoted to "The Rôle of Socialization in Social Progress," and in about a hundred pages it presented the best review or epitome of social development which had been thus far produced by an American sociologist. It suggested and described four main stages of social development and socialization: (1) the kinship stage; (2) the personal-feudal stage; (3) the personal-town stage; and (4) the impersonal stage.

If Giddings never reduced his lectures on social evolution and the history of civilization to print, one of his foremost students, F. Stuart Chapin, produced two books which were inspired by Giddings and reproduced something of the spirit and content of Giddings' teachings in this field. These were *An Introduction to the Study of Social Evolution* (1913), and *An Historical Introduction to Social Economy* (1917). They remained for some years the best survey of historical sociology and social history by an American scholar. Some of this material was later embodied, along with a great deal more theoretical discussion, in Chapin's *Cultural Change,* which also reflected the influence of the cultural approach to historical sociology as emphasized by Boas, Marett, Kroeber and the cultural anthropologists. Ellwood's *Cultural Evolution,* which we have previously mentioned, was in part devoted to theories of cultural and social evolution and in part to a study of the origin and development of certain phases of culture and leading social institutions. It offered a panorama of the stages in the evolution of culture and society, based on Morgan's *Ancient Society* and Alexander Sutherland's *Origin and Growth of the Moral Instinct.*

One of the most important American contributions to the theory of cultural change and social evolution came not from the pen of a sociologist but from an historian, Frederick J. Teggart, and was embodied in his three books: *Prolegomena to History* (1916); *The Processes of History* (1918); and *Theory of History* (1925).[14] In these books Teggart sought to combine the accuracy of the documentary, narrative historians with the evolutionary sweep of the sociologists. Historians have achieved accuracy, but their narratives are often lacking in significance for those who wish to understand the course of social and cultural evolution, while sociologists and evolutionists are wont to formulate grandiose conceptions of social development which have little regard for specific facts. By applying the scientific method to historical data, Teggart sought to discover the constants and determinants in historical sequences and cultural evolution, especially in regard to political development.

Teggart's first book formulated the problem of the scientific study of cultural development; the second examined the relative influence of human and geographic factors, stressing the importance of geographic forces in unifying history and of human migrations in producing changes and cultural advances; and the third dealt mainly with methods of studying social evolution—Hume's psychological approach; Turgot's idea of the continuity of history; and the impact of the doctrine of evolution upon notions of social change. In his *The Processes of History*, Teggart anticipated very definitely Toynbee's notions of challenge and response and creative individual initiative. In Teggart's interpretation, the most dynamic factor in history is the migration of peoples and the inter-communication of social groups. This stimulates the conflict of social ideas which, in time, brings about an abandonment of tradition and conventional doctrines and opens the way to new vistas of thought and to social innovations. Teggart's main weakness was his lack of command of up-to-date sociology.

The American scholar who probably possesses the most complete mastery of the facts of anthropology and social evolution requisite to produce a systematic history of human society is William Christie MacLeod, well trained as an anthropologist, sociologist and economist. His only extended work on historical sociology thus far published is his *The Origin and History of Politics* (1931), which traces the evolution of the main forms of political society from primitive tribalism to Fascist and Soviet totalitarianism.

American scholars have been far more prolific in producing social history than in writing systematic treatises in the field of historical sociology. James T. Shotwell, who was closely associated with Giddings, did much to stimulate interest in this field but he never published anything substantial along this line. The writer's *History of Western Civilization* (1935) is the most comprehensive American synthesis of social history. Comparable works in more specialized fields are Ralph Turner's magisterial synthesis of ancient civilization in his *The Great Cultural Traditions* (1941), Michael I. Roztovtzev's voluminous works on the social and economic history of Greek, Hellenistic and Roman times, James Westfield Thompson's masterly volumes on the social and economic history of the Middle Ages, and the four-volume work of Charles Austin and Mary Beard on American social and intellectual history. But, while social history is indispensable as a basis for historical sociology, it is not, as Howard Becker has properly pointed out, the same thing as historical sociology, which embodies a more theoretical and generalized approach to the history of human society.

1. Barnes *et al., op. cit.,* Chap. XXVII; for a sympathetic interpretation and estimate of Durkheim, see Lowie, *op. cit.,* pp. 197–212; for a critical analysis, see Alexander Goldenweiser, *op. cit.,* pp. 361–376.
2. Lowie, *op. cit.,* pp. 230–242.
3. London, 1915; written in collaboration with G. C. Wheeler and Morris Ginsberg.
4. *Journal of the Royal Anthropological Institute,* XVIII (1889), 245–272.
5. Hobhouse, *op. cit.,* pp. 1–2.
6. Wilhelm Schmidt, *The Culture Historical Method of Ethnology* (New York: Fortuny's, 1939), pp. 54–58; Barnes and Becker, *Contemporary Social Theory,* Chap. 5, and pp. 500, 511, 516.
7. Barnes and Becker, *Contemporary Social Theory,* Chap. 15.
8. *Ibid.,* pp. 517–522; and Barnes and Becker, *Social Thought from Lore to Science,* Vol. I, pp. 769–781.
9. Barnes *et al., op. cit.,* Chap. XIII.
10. *Ibid.,* Chap. XVII; and Barnes and Becker, *Social Thought from Lore to Science,* Vol. I, pp. 771–777.
11. Lowie, *op. cit.,* Chap. IX. For a list of leading anthropologists who have adopted a critical and scientific attitude, outside the immediate Boas circle, see Goldenweiser, *op cit.,* p. 83, footnote 2.
12. White, *op. cit., Journal of the Washington Academy of Sciences,* XXXVII (June 15, 1947), pp. 210, 214.
13. See C. A. Beard's Introduction to Adams, *op. cit.* (New York: Knopf, 1943).
14. Goldenweiser, *op. cit.,* pp. 89–110.

CHAPTER V

THE IMPORTANCE OF THEORIES OF CULTURAL EVOLUTION FOR HISTORICAL SOCIOLOGY

We have several times referred to the conception, going back as far as Tylor and Lippert, that culture factors and institutional evolution are independent of biological laws and processes and that historical sociology is essentially a science of culture. This position was most effectively established by the cultural anthropologists, such as Marett and the Boas school. The most important bearing which cultural anthropology has upon historical sociology relates to the theories, laws and processes governing the origin and growth of cultural traits and social institutions. To this matter we may now turn briefly.[1]

The cultural anthropologists have advanced some four chief doctrines or explanations of cultural growth and change: (1) the independent origins and unilateral evolution of culture and institutions, the same the world over; (2) limited inventiveness and the diffusion of cultural traits, through actual contact of different cultures, by means of imitation; (3) the convergence of cultural traits towards uniformity due to the limited range and possibilities of cultural and institutional patterns; and (4) the derivation of cultural patterns and institutions from the functional needs of the human organism, which assures relative similarity.

The first theory was that expounded by the evolutionary and comparative school, namely the theory of the *independent origins* and parallel development of cultural patterns, due to the basic unity of the human mind, as postulated by Bastian, and to environmental similarities. Changes in social institutions are, likewise, usually due to causes arising independent of any other social group or culture. This doctrine, of course, embodied the apotheosis of human initiative and capacity for invention and left little place or rôle for imitation through cultural contacts.

At the opposite pole from this school of writers was that group which accounted for cultural growth, parallelisms, and transformations on the basis of cultural contacts, imitation and *diffusion.* They held that the instances of invention and independent origins of culture are very few, indeed, and that changes in culture are due almost entirely to the introduction of new cultural traits or elements from outside by means of contacts between social groups. This view of cultural development was anticipated by Tylor, Friedrich Ratzel, Lippert and Heinrich Schurtz, and was elaborated by Leo Frobenius, Fritz Graebner, Willy Foy, G. Elliott Smith, and W. J. Perry. It was adopted by Bernhard Ankermann, W. H. R. Rivers, Wilhelm Schmidt, Wilhelm Koppers and Clyde Cluckhorn. Even Clark Wissler, often regarded as a leading member of the Boas school, adopted a moderate version of diffusionism. While possessing considerable validity, especially as an explanation of the spread of material culture, the diffusion hypothesis has many weaknesses from psychological and geographical viewpoints. Extremists, like Perry, have claimed imitation and diffusion of culture as between peoples who apparently could not possibly have had any direct or indirect contacts at the time involved.

Recognizing the defects of both of these older theories, Felix von Luschan and Ehrenreich in Germany, Marett in England, and Boas and his school in America have substituted a critical or historico-analytical procedure. They assign full credit to the theory of independent development and invention as the cause of many cultural origins and changes, but also recognize that diffusion is a very important factor in accounting for cultural progress and transformations.

Particularly significant is the searching analysis of alleged cultural parallelisms which has been carried on by this group from the historical and psychological point of view. They have satisfactorily proved that many alleged parallelisms are similar only in superficial externals and are not identical in their psychic or cultural content or their historical development. They have, further, demonstrated that actual parallelisms and similarities may have developed from quite different origins through the operation of the principle of "convergence" in the growth of culture. By *convergence* is meant the tendency of separate developmental processes in culture to culminate in very similar types or features, even though they may have originally appeared quite independently and followed for a time a disparate course of growth. Goldenweiser has pointed out that, due to the bio-psychic nature of man and the character of his physical environment, the types of material culture, social institutions and group beliefs are inevitably limited. Hence, we naturally will find similarities in culture and institutions without any contacts whatever. The revolutionary significance of such positions in the interpretation of cultural evolution cannot fail to be obvious to any thoughtful historian or sociologist.

Another type of explanation of cultural innovations and similarities, which minimizes the controversy between independent development, diffusion and convergence, is what is known as the functional interpretation of culture which has been upheld by Richard Thurnwald, A. R. Radcliffe-Brown and, especially, by Malinowski in his *A Scientific Theory of Culture*. According to this doctrine, cultural phenomena do not arise and develop primarily from inevitable and universal inventiveness or from imitation through cultural contacts and borrowing (diffusion). They are a product of the basic needs of the human organism in its social setting. These functional needs and the different habitats and social systems in which peoples seek their satisfaction are sufficient to account for the origin, variety and development of cultural traits. It is but a step from the functional approach to the interest in the relation between personality and culture, an approach founded by men like Paul Radin, which has attracted a good deal of attention recently on the part of anthropologists.

Inasmuch as most historical sociologists have, until recently, adhered to the evolutionary and comparative method of studying social genesis, they naturally accepted the basic tenet of this school on the subject of cultural evolution, namely, the theory of independent origins and development. Those members of the present generation of sociologists who are familiar with at least the general methods and conclusions of the cultural anthropologists have paid attention to all these principles of independent development, diffusion and convergence. Most of them now adhere to the doctrines of the Boas school, but they have rarely gone deeply into ethnological theory. As Howard Becker has truthfully said, they have usually done little more than shift their allegiance from Morgan and evolutionary anthropology to Boas and his conceptions.

At any rate, these conceptions of cultural and institutional development are of more than academic or dialectical significance for historical sociology. They constitute the main basis for deriving the laws, trends and principles of institutional development which is a main task of historical sociology. For years, the historical sociologists relied upon the laws of biological growth or the dogmas of Spencerian cosmic evolution to give them the clue to social evolution, its laws and principles. Since we now admit that social and cultural facts are primarily "superorganic," and have ceased to interpret social evolution in terms of the formulas of cosmic evolution, the principles of cultural evolution furnish the main source of guidance for the historical sociologist in his theorizing about social genesis. But any complete schedule or category of the laws and principles of cultural evolution must await further development of culturology. Hence, the historical sociologists may well extend their encouragement to those who, like Professor White, are engaged in this enterprise.

---

1. On theories of cultural evolution, see Lowie, *op. cit.*, pp. 27–29, 72 ff., 122ff., 156–195; Goldenweiser, *op. cit.*, Parts I-II; Schmidt, *op. cit.*, *passim;* Effie Bendann, *Death Customs* (New York: Knopf, 1930), pp. 1–18; R. B. Dixon, *The Building of Cultures* (New York: Scribner's, 1928); Barnes, *History and Prospects of the Social Sciences,* Chap. V., and Barnes and Becker, *Contemporary Social Theory,* Chap. 14.

PART II

What Historical Sociology Has Contributed to Our Knowledge of the History of Human Society

CHAPTER VI

SOCIOLOGICAL CONTRIBUTIONS TO OUR KNOWL-EDGE OF SOCIAL AND POLITICAL EVOLUTION

I. THE STAGES OF SOCIAL EVOLUTION

Thus far, we have devoted our attention mainly to the methods and principles embodied in historical sociology as exemplified by leading schools of sociological and anthropological thought and the writers therein. We may appropriately continue our survey with a summary of some of the leading contributions which sociologists have made to our knowledge of the social development of mankind.

One of the most illuminating and valuable of the phases of historical sociology has been the effort of writers in this field from various points of view to distinguish, characterize, or mark off the major stages in social evolution. The first epoch-making attempt along this line was the work of Auguste Comte. Comte did not rest satisfied, as so many have contended, with a purely intellectual theory of social evolution. His famous division of history into the theological, metaphysical, and positive stages applied merely to his notion of intellectual progress. His stages of social evolution were based upon a more comprehensive set of factors. His complete demarcation of the stages in the history of society included a theological-military period, a metaphysical-legalistic age, and the modern scientific-industrial era. Herbert Spencer believed that the chief social transformation thus far achieved has been the shift from a society organized primarily for war to one oriented chiefly for industrial purposes, this change being accompanied by a progressive decline in state activity. He risked the generalization that a third period might be attained in which ethical and social considerations would play a dominating part. Walter Bagehot held that the three chief periods of social and cultural evolution have been: (1) that of the formation of codes of local custom, (2) that of the struggle of local groups dominated by customary codes, with the resulting formation of states, and, finally, (3) that of the dissolution of the domination of custom by the appearance of the age of discussion. Kovalevsky contended that the chief stages in social evolution are: (1) the period of the horde and the matrilineal family; (2) the era of the gens and the transition to the paternal family; (3) patriarchal nomadism; (4) feudalism; and (5) democracy. In his *Elements of Folk Psychology,* Wilhelm Wundt maintained that there are four great successive culture eras in the evolution of mankind: (1) the period of primitive man; (2) the period of totemism; (3) the period of gods and heroes; and (4) the period of humanity. Durkheim has viewed social evolution as primarily the passage from a social system based upon a mechanical and constraining solidarity produced by group repression of individuality to a social system founded upon the organic and voluntary solidarity of the social division of labor and the functional organization of society.

Guillaume DeGreef asserted that the history of society can be most intelligently summed up as the transformation from a régime based upon force to one characterized by voluntary and contractual social relationships. Jacques Novicow contended that social evolution is a process of substituting progressively higher for lower forms of social conflict. The serial sequence of these basic types or periods of social conflict have been from the physiological, through the economic and the political, to the intellectual, or highest form of social conflict. Gustav Ratzenhofer and Albion W. Small have suggested that the most vital social transformation has been that from a "conquest-state" to a "culture-state," carrying with it the realization of a progressively more adequate range of social interests. Ferdinand Tönnies built up his system of sociology around the transition from community and mental inertia to society and mental mobility. L. T. Hobhouse held that the stages of social and political evolution have been those in which kinship, authority, and citizenship have, in order, been the basis of social cohesion and political organization.

By far the most thorough and illuminating scheme for organizing the evolution of society is that which was suggested by Giddings. He divided social evolution into the following stages: *Zoögenic*, or animal society; *Anthropogenic*, or the society of man in the stage of the transformation from animal to human tribal society; *Ethnogenic*, or tribal socety; and *Demogenic*, or the so-called "historic" period. This last era he further divided into the Military-religious period, which roughly corresponds to that of oriental antiquity, and the early Middle Ages; the Liberal-legal period, or that of Greece and Rome and early modern history; and the Economic-ethical period, or that since the Industrial Revolution.

Ellwood added to Morgan's three-fold division of Savage and Barbarian stages a third tripartite stage of "Civilized Peoples," namely, the Lower Civilized, including the achievements we usually associate with Ancient and Medieval history; the Middle Civilized, involving developments from early modern times to the nineteenth century; and the Upper Civilized, or those nations which have participated in the culture of our mechanized Western world.[1]

While these characterizations of the outstanding stages or periods in social evolution differ somewhat, they are not mutually exclusive, but reflect varied points of view and widely diverse methods of studying the history of society. They constitute one of the most significant phases, both of the development of historical sociology and of the contribution of sociology to history.

Perhaps the most prolific contribution to the attempt to work out stages in institutional evolution was made by economic historians, such as Karl Bücher. A characteristic product of this type of theorizing would summarize economic development in the following stages:

The economy of collectors—natural foraging, hunting and fishing.
The pastoral economy.
The agricultural economy.
The commercial economy.
The industrial economy.
The financial economy.
The governmental economy—state capitalism or state socialism.

This type of work is well surveyed and analyzed in Chapter III of Part I of Richard T. Ely's *Studies in the Evolution of Industrial Society* (1903).

II. THE SOCIO-PSYCHOLOGICAL BASIS OF THE ORIGINS OF HUMAN ASSOCIATION AND POLITICAL AUTHORITY

A complete sociological theory of the origin of civil society involves a consideration of the following problems: (1) the socio-psychological origins of human association in the most general terms; (2) the sociological and psychological forces involved in the origins of political consolidation and leadership; (3) the nature and progress of political organization in tribal society; and (4) the causes for and nature of the rise of the territorial state.

The sociological doctrines that have been adduced to explain the origins and nature of human association are numerous and varied, but they are rarely contradictory, and the final synthesis of sociological doctrine will, in all probability, accord in different degrees recognition to all of them. It will suffice here to mention some of the more important views of the better-known sociologists.

In such a category would belong the theories of sympathy from Adam Smith to Alexander Sutherland; the closely allied doctrine of mutual aid and spontaneous coöperation, set forth by such writers as Prince Kropotkin and Novicow; the notion of a gregarious instinct, as elaborated by William McDougall and Wilfred Trotter; Giddings' emphasis on the "consciousness of kind"; the effect of imitation expounded by David Hume, Bagehot, Gabriel Tarde, and James Mark Baldwin; the subordination of the individual by the impressive force of the group, as viewed by Durkheim, Gustave LeBon, Scipio Sighele, Gumplowicz, and Sumner; and John Fiske's theory of the prolongation of human infancy.

The socio-psychological explanations of the rise of political superiority and subordination are closely allied to these interpretations of the origins of all associated life. We have Spencer's doctrine of fear; Bagehot's and Tarde's theory of imitation; DeGreef's and Alfred Fouillée's versions of the theory of political origins through self-interest and a voluntary contract; Kropotkin's and Novicow's stressing of coöperative activity; Durkheim's and LeBon's insistence upon the influence of group impression on the individual mind; W. H. Mallock's, Georges Sorel's Emile Faguet's, Eben Mumford's, Gaetano Mosca's, and Vilfredo Pareto's exposition of the significance of leadership and dominating personalities; McDougall's theory of an instinct of self-abasement and an emotion of subjection; the notions of Gumplowicz, Ratzenhofer and Small relative to the conflict and adjustment of social interests; the attempt to reach a synthetic interpretation in Giddings' notion of differential response to

stimulation and the theory of protocracy; and the well-balanced
doctrine of Baldwin, C. H. Cooley and Ellwood.

III. THE RISE OF SOCIAL AND POLITICAL INSTITUTIONS

The first modern attempt to trace the historical development
of political origins during the period of tribal society rested on
the theory which was supposed to be of biblical origin and
sanction and had been confirmed by the generalizations of
Aristotle, Bodin, Pufendorf, Locke, and Blackstone, namely,
that the patriarchal organization of society had been the earliest
form of family, social, and political life.[2] This thesis received
its ablest synthesis and defense in the *Ancient Law* (1861) and
other monumental contributions to comparative jurisprudence
and politics from the pen of Sir Henry Sumner Maine (1822–
1888). Yet, as Lowie has done well to point out, Maine was no
fanatical partisan of patriarchalism. Indeed, he denied that the
patriarchal family had been universal in primitive society. He
stressed patriarchalism because his work dealt mainly with early
Indo-Germanic society which had been organized on a patriarchal basis.

The patriarchal thesis was attacked by Johann Jacob Bachofen
(1815–1887) in his *Das Mutterrecht* published in 1861. He
maintained the existence of a primordial promiscuity in sexual
relations and a subsequent development of a matriarchate, or
a polity dominated by females. But he was a follower of the
methods of Vico and Wolf rather than those of Darwin and
Morgan, for he based his generalizations upon data drawn from
a study of classical mythology and tradition.

This rather archaic line of approach was soon abandoned for
what has come to be known as the "evolutionary" approach to
historical sociology. A group of distinguished scholars, most
notable among them being Sir John Lubbock, J. F. McLennan,

Herbert Spencer, Andrew Lang, W. Robertson Smith, Albert H. Post, Edward B. Tylor, Lewis H. Morgan, James G. Frazer, Charles Letourneau, and Daniel G. Brinton, as we have seen, brought evolutionary principles and Darwinian biology to bear upon the reconstruction of the early history of human society and also reached results which appeared to be disruptive of the patriarchal position of Maine. While there were important differences of opinion in matters of detail among these writers, they were in general agreement upon the essentials of method and in the results of their work. The leading special assailant of the patriarchal theory among this group was John Ferguson McLennan (1827–1881), whose ideas were developed in his *Primitive Marriage* (1865) ; *Studies in Ancient History* (1876) ; and his posthumous, *The Patriarchal Theory* (1885).

Applying their methods and assumptions, described elsewhere, to the study of early society, these writers arrived at a series of definite conclusions: the monogamous family shows a slow but distinct development from original promiscuity, and the family of any conscious type is a late product, developing within the kinship or gentile organization of society. In the development of gentile society certain definite and successive stages can be isolated and their sequence correlated with the development of material culture. The first type of extensive human grouping was found in the endogamous horde, where there were neither fixed family arrangements nor other wider relations. This stage was followed by the appearance of definite kinship or gentile society, associated with the exogamous clan, which was almost inseparably connected with a totemic complex. It was McLennan who invented the terms endogamy and exogamy. The earliest form of gentile society was the maternal clan, which was in time succeeded by the paternal clan, or gens, this transformation in the basis of relationships being definitely correlated with progressive advances in material culture. The paternal clan or gens gradually evolved into a patriarchal organization of society, which, through the development of property and the infiltration of foreigners from economic attraction, was in time superseded by the abolition of kinship relations and the establishment of the territorial state and civil society. This orderly synthesis of social and political evolution was, as we have noted, most comprehensively organized and most effectively set forth in the famous work on *Ancient Society* by Morgan.

Since Morgan's day new methods of anthropological investigation and synthesis and more thorough studies of existing primitive society have, as noted above, served to discredit the methods of investigation followed by the evolutionary or classical school of anthropologists and to disprove many conclusions which they reached by the employment of these methods. In fact, even more careful investigation following the older methods enabled Westermarck to prove inaccurate the assumption of primitive promiscuity.

The basis for the newer point of view was laid by many painstaking studies of primitive culture areas in the attempt to investigate the data in an objective manner. Space forbids the mention of more than a few representative examples of this type of indispensable anthropological research.[3] In any such enumeration we would have to include the studies of Australian data by C. Strehlow, H. Cunow, G. G. Brown, and N. W. Thomas; Rivers' great monograph on the Todas, and his *History of Melanesian Society;* C. G. Seligman's survey of the Veddas; the Torres Straits investigations undertaken by A. C. Haddon, Rivers, and a group of English scholars; Malinowski's studies of the natives of the Pacific islands; the investigation of African data by J. Roscoe, E. Pechuël-Loesche and M. J. Herskovits; and especially the careful studies of primitive American culture areas by Boas, Wissler, Lowie, Kroeber, Goldenweiser, Edward Sapir, H. J. Spinden, A. C. Parker, Dixon,

Leslie Spier, Pliny Goddard, James Mooney, F. G. Speck, J. R. Swanton, Truman Michelson, and others.

This unprecedented body of accurate data, together with a more objective and scientific attitude toward its interpretation, has not only brought about more reliable ideas concerning social evolution, but has also shown that the facts of social development are far different from what was earlier supposed. The more critical school has proved that the assumption of a universal law of evolution from the simple to the complex is not invariably true with respect to culture or social institutions. It has shown that parallelisms in culture and social organization in different areas do not imply identical antecedents or necessarily bring about the same subsequent developments. Similarities may grow out of "cultural convergencies," proceeding from widely varied antecedents or they may be produced by imitation of a common pattern.

The application of this more scientific method to the study of primitive society has been nothing short of revolutionary.[4] The universality of gentile or kinship society cannot be proved; many groups have developed to a relatively high stage of culture without any relationship system wider than the family and the local group. Where gentile society exists there is no general tendency for relationships to change from a maternal to a paternal basis; in fact, it may be doubted if there is one well-authenticated example of an independent change in kinship from a maternal to a paternal basis in the whole range of primitive society. Further, there is no evidence that maternal kinship is correlated with lower material culture or paternal with more advanced economic life. Finally, totemism has been dissociated from exogamy. It is evident that much of the pattern of social evolution provided by the evolutionary school has been discredited and Robert H. Lowie has well expressed the obituary notice of this school:

To sum up. There is no fixed succession of maternal and paternal descent; sibless tribes may pass directly into the matrilineal or the patrilineal condition; if the highest civilizations emphasize the paternal side of the family, so do many of the lowest; and the social history of any particular people cannot be reconstructed from any generally valid scheme of social evolution but only in the light of its known and probable cultural relations with neighboring peoples.[5]

These more critical principles and more assured results in anthropological research have, as we have pointed out, been chiefly an American product and associated with the work of Franz Boas and his pupils, but mention should be made of such Europeans as Marett, Rivers, von Luschan, Ehrenreich, Thurnwald, Vierkandt, M. Haberlandt, and others.

The next problem in the sociological theory of political origins centers around tracing the origin of the developed territorial state. Older views, following Aristotle, regarded it as a natural expansion of social groupings from tribal to civil society. Morgan and the evolutionary school accounted for political origins on the basis of the rise of property and the necessity of a more advanced type of political and legal institutions to cope with these more complex economic problems. Gradually, however, the doctrine has gained ground that the territorial state was primarily the product of forcible subjugation through long-continued warfare among primitive groups. Today, this may be said to be *the* sociological theory of political origins and development. This view is not a new one; as we have seen, it certainly may be traced back as far as Polybius and has had its exponents in every succeeding age. Bodin, Hume, in his *Essays,* and Adam Ferguson in his *History of Civil Society* may be regarded as the founders of the modern version of this doctrine. Spencer and Bagehot worked over the doctrine in the light of evolutionary concepts, but it is with the work of Ludwig Gumplowicz and his theory of the *Rassenkampf* that this important contribution to the sociological theory of the state is usually associated. Gumplowicz forecast this interpretation in his brochure on *Rasse und Staat* in 1875 and expanded it in two later works, *Der Rassenkampf* (1883), and *Grundriss der Soziologie* (1885). It has been taken up and elaborated, among others, by Ratzenhofer in Austria, Oppenheimer and Georg Simmel in Germany, Edward Jenks in England, and Small and Ward in America. Since we have already summarized this conception of the origin of the state in treating Social Darwinism we shall not repeat it at this point.

Though this view of political origins has received the general assent of most sociologists, some have vigorously criticized it as minimizing the element of coöperation and other peaceful agencies, such as industry and trade, which have undoubtedly been potent factors in the history of the state. Among the better known of such writers have been Sutherland in his *Origin and Growth of the Moral Instinct,* Kropotkin in his *Mutual Aid as a Factor in Evolution,* and Novicow in his *La Critique du Darwinisme social.*[6] Eclectic writers have tried to work out a synthesis and to show that, while conflict played the dominant rôle in political origins, coöperative activities have not been without great influence in the past and will probably be even more powerful in the future. Such a point of view has characterized the doctrine of Giddings, E. C. Hayes, Ludwig Stein, and Tarde.

IV. STAGES AND TYPES IN SOCIO-POLITICAL EVOLUTION

Sociologists have not only dealt with social and political origins; they have traced the whole course of social and political evolution. We may here summarize the results of such studies.

First, humanity was organized, for the most part, on what has been called the gentile basis, namely, tribal society, in which the individual's position and the power of the rulers were founded upon blood relationship, real or assumed. One did not have rights or prestige because he resided in a certain place or because he was protected by some overlord. He owed all his status and privileges to the fact that he was a member of a quasi-biological clan or gens that was believed to be composed of blood brethren, irrespective of whether the relationship was traced through the male or the female line. An interloper had no rights or privileges. Those who ruled were elected by and from the blood brethren. Even such elaborate political organizations in primitive society as the Iroquois tribes and confederacy rested fundamentally on clan units that were made up of alleged kinsmen. The same was true of even the early Germanic tribes when they first appeared on the historical horizon. Real or fictitious blood relationship, then, was the foundation of primitive political organization, though family relations and local propinquity served occasionally to hold men together and secure public order.

In the frequent and numerous wars that took place during the interval between primitive and historic civil society, some of these kinship groups were conquered and reconquered by others and subjected to the rule of the victors. Blood relationships were thus gradually obscured and broken down. In this age of conquest, personal loyalty to dominant personalities became more and more important. The basis for public control was the loyal support of the leader by his followers and the protection of his subordinates by the leader. In short, personal relationships, founded on superiority and subordination, on loyalty and protection, supplanted the blood-kinship basis of primitive society. The resulting political and social order was what we know as feudalism. This rudimentary feudal system seems to have existed as the background of most early historical political societies, intervening between primitive tribal organization and the more highly developed political state, grounded in territorial residence and property rights. Early city-states and monarchies thus appear to have arisen out of feudal origins. This feudal order reappeared again in western civilization when the Greek and Roman social structure collapsed, and the northern barbarians gained control of public affairs in Western Europe. This medieval feudalism is the best-known example of the feudal system.

The earliest type of political organization which rested upon a territorial and property basis was the city-state that appeared first in Egypt and Mesopotamia more than five millennia before Christ. It persisted in various forms and areas down to the rise of imperial Rome, though earlier empires had sporadically blotted it out in wide sections of the ancient East. Indeed, city-state culture was revived in early modern Italy, Germany, and Holland. The Greek city-state was perhaps the highest development attained by this form of politico-social organization. Antiquity produced not only the city-state but also the kingdom and the patriarchal empire, welded by the conquest of many scattered city-states. But neither the city-state, the kingdom, nor the empire brought about a truly national psychology or political organization. The city-state was too small and provincial. The kingdoms and empires were too vast, embraced too many peoples and cultures, or were of too brief duration to weld their divergent cultures into a national unit. Even the Roman Empire did not attain a national, self-conscious character.

The political, social, economic, and cultural conditions of the Middle Ages were no better adapted to the creation of the national state than were those of imperial antiquity. The unit of political organization and administration was the domain of the feudal lord. This varied greatly in area, but rarely was it coextensive with any cultural or national entity. Usually a single feudal domain was but a small isolated element in the feudal hierarchy, and it made for political decentralization and local immunity rather than for national unity. Medieval social life centered in each of the large number of isolated and minute medieval manors and in each of the few small and scattered medieval towns. The units of agrarian and urban industry, the manors and the towns respectively, were relatively isolated, nearly self-sufficient, and narrowly selfish and provincial. They were thoroughly unadapted to providing any firm economic foundations for national unity. The pivotal points in medieval culture were the royal palaces, towns and the monasteries. The kings were too few, too poorly connected by means of communication, and too much governed by the spirit of localism and jealous isolation to be able to bring into being to any marked extent that general cultural homogeneity so all-essential to the existence of national unity. Nor were the monasteries any better suited to promote naional spirit.

Not until early modern times do we arrive at the point where a new political entity of great import for the future of humanity emerges, namely, the national state.

The feudal order was characterized, above everything else, by localism and the immunity of the feudal lord. The center of political power was the feudal domain, and only the most tenuous authority inhered in the average feudal monarch. Such power as he did have was primarily derived from his own position as a strong feudal lord and from the aid given him by his subordinate feudal lords. The stronger kings of the feudal period owed their power chiefly to the creation of some sort of royal army. Each feudal lord was supreme in his own domain, and he was immune from higher control after he had met his duties and obligations to his overlords and king. Feudalism was an institutional testimonial to the relative unimportance of the nonlocal and impersonal aspects of life.

With rise of the national state after 1400 all this was thoroughly transformed. Political power became centralized, first in monarchs and later in elective rulers. The state became absolute, and all too often it crushed out at will the immunities and privileges of individuals, whether lords or common men. The authority and administration radiated from the center of the realm, instead of being scattered about in outlying regions. The kings hired their own armies and administration, instead of relying on levies of feudal troops and the administration of justice by feudal lords. Order was preserved by the monarch; his will had to be respected by all under his dominion. National sovereignty supplanted local immunity. Order gradually grew out of chaos.

During the decline of feudalism at the close of the medieval period, the stronger feudal monarchs were beginning to assert their power at the expense of the feudal lords and to lay the foundation of the national monarchy. This movement was hastened by the expansion of Europe and the Commercial Revolution, after 1500, which brought into play forces which served to extinguish the political aspects of feudalism and to create a system of nationalism. The expansion of Europe gave the kings more money to hire loyal armies and administrators. The ascendancy of infantry made it cheaper and easier to hire efficient mercenary armies. The middle-class lawyers and other functionaries provided the kings with the administrative bureaucracy that the new centralized governments required.

This process of building the national state first appeared in the form of absolute monarchy; and then absolutism was undermined by the growth of revolutionary doctrines and the rise of representative government. Republics proved no less nationalistic than the earlier monarchies. Political liberalism has not yet consistently produced cosmopolitanism or internationalism. The democracies in the twentieth century remained as nationalistic as seventeenth-century monarchies. The greatest wars of the nations were fought in the second and fifth decades of our own century, and democratic states entered them with as much ardor and as little provocation as the most reactionary empires or the most ruthless totalitarian states.

The outstanding trend in political evolution since the Middle Ages was, thus, the rise of the national state. It was at first monarchical and tyrannical, then it was slowly adapted to representative government, and, finally, in the 19th and 20th centuries, it became democratic in most countries in the western world.

In our day, however, nationalism has proved quite inadequate to the institutional conditions brought into being by the urban, industrial world-civilization that has been created by three Industrial Revolutions. The national state now threatens mankind with devastating bellicosity, and has created a centralized political unity in juxtaposition with public problems that may be too vast and complex to be solved through democracy and party government.

The experience of the last generation has made realists aware that whatever virtues nationalism may have, they certainly do not warrant the perpetuation of any system which invites (or even provokes) successive world wars and the imperiling of all civilization. The problem has arisen of how to provide some more rational form of political organization than the national state, and at the same time to protect any traits and manifestations of nationalism which are of any demonstrable and permanent value to mankind. The most popular and sensible program of political readjustment, which would involve the control, though not necessarily the total suppression, of nationalism is what is called regionalism.

Regionalism is a somewhat loose and confused conception because many different ideas are included under this term. Some regionalists have in mind, at least for the time being, no more than an economic union, like the German *Zollverein*. Others urge a strong and highly centralized federation of former national states. Some regionalists envisage the unification of a relatively small area—some natural organic portion of a continent or group of islands. Others contemplate no less than continental federal unions. Indeed, some would include within regional organization a structure as vast as the western hemisphere.

Representative government produced political parties as the agency to provide representatives. Representation has been based upon population, resident within a given territorial district. But party government is breaking down in our day. Political corruption has paralyzed the conventional party system. Political blocs bring anarchy to party government. The other extreme, the one-party system, is the formula and technique of totalitarian systems. The reform of representative and party government has become an outstanding problem of our era.

One suggestion is to abandon the principle of representation by territorial districts and population and base it upon the vital occupational and professional groups in modern society. It is claimed that, since each district contains many interests, even the most conflicting interests, no one elected representative can logically or competently represent his whole district in a legislature. If, however, the leading interest-groups or vocations were to elect their representatives directly, those who were thus elected could honestly and competently represent those who elected them. The argument is that such a system would produce superior representatives, since no interest-group would take the chance of being represented by a venal, ignorant, or incompetent man. And this method would also eliminate the evil of the lobby, since all interests could be directly represented.

There is much to support the force and logic of this proposition but it runs counter to the older democratic idea that representative government must be based upon geographical districts and upon numerical representation and majority decisions. Great confusion might arise as to the distribution of power and numerical representation among the various interest-groups. Vocational representation has been tried in different degrees in Europe, but it has never been installed except as the result of revolution or war.

The following brief outline recapitulates the main stages in the political evolution of mankind:

I. Tribal society
    Kinship basis
    Personal relations in politics
II. The transitional stage of feudalism
    Personal bonds in social organization
    Quasi-territorial basis of politics
    Rise of property in political considerations
III. The territorial state and civil society
    City-states
    Patriarchal empires of antiquity
    The national state
        Absolutistic
        Representative
        Democratic (usually republican)
IV. The functional and regional political society of the future
    Political federations, and spheres of interest
    Functional or vocational representation

A large number of sociologists have contributed to the elaboration of this panorama of political evolution. Among them the most notable have been Gumplowicz, Oppenheimer, Ratzenhofer, Ludwig Stein, Hans Fryer, Kovalevsky, Novicow, Durkheim, Robert Michels, Hobhouse, Sumner, Giddings and MacLeod.[7] In my *Sociology and Political Theory* (1924) I have summarized the main contributions of sociologists to the interpretation of political evolution and political processes.

1. C. A. Ellwood, *Cultural Evolution* (New York: Century, 1927), Chap. II.
2. Lowie, *op. cit.,* Chap. V.
3. Lowie, *op. cit.,* pp. 131–136, 148–151; Goldenweiser, *op. cit.,* p. 83, footnote 2.
4. R. H. Lowie, *Primitive Society* (New York: Boni, 1920).
5. Lowie, *Primitive Society,* p. 185.
6. Barnes *et al., op. cit.,* Chap. XXII.
7. W. C. MacLeod, *The Origin and History of Politics,* Wiley, 1931.

CHAPTER VII

INTERPRETATIONS OF SOCIAL EVOLUTION ON THE GRAND SCALE

I. BROOKS ADAMS: FROM BARBARISM TO CIVILIZATION AND BACK TO BARBARISM

The contributions of historical sociologists to the description of social evolution may be divided logically into two types. First we have the efforts to work out ambitious interpretations of the course of civilization from early times until our own—more or less complete syntheses of social development. The second type constitute special studies of successive eras in the history of mankind. We may first turn our attention to the more general type of synthesis of social evolution.

Probably the first American contribution to a broad review of social evolution which we can regard as historical sociology was embodied in *The Law of Civilization and Decay* by Brooks Adams, to which we have already made reference. Brooks apparently made a philosopher out of his brother Henry and stimulated the latter's well-known effort to interpret history in terms of thermo-dynamics.[1]

Brooks Adams' philosophy of history was built up gradually as a result of a number of lines of thought. His original and daring study of colonial New England impressed him with the hitherto generally neglected economic factors in the Protestant Reformation. Reflecting upon the then-popular Darwinism and Spencerianism, Adams became skeptical of the dogma of universal and unilateral progress. The dramatic importance and immediacy of financial and monetary problems in the early 'nineties, emphasized the potent rôle of capitalism and finance throughout the course of history.

Adams' conception of the evolution and destiny of human civilization may be briefly summarized about as follows: The history of mankind is, in the most profound sense, the human manifestation of dynamic cosmic energy. The actions of all animal societies, including the human race, are refined and secondary expressions of solar energy. The historical evolution of our race and human culture constitutes a social progression from Barbarism (dispersion) to Civilization (concentration), and then a reversion to Barbarism and Anarchy.

In the case of the human race, cosmic energy expresses itself chiefly through mental activity. In the era of Barbarism, Fear is the dominating mental trait and it produced the imaginative mind. This manifests itself in war, conquest and other deeds of virility, in notable works of art, and in the storing up of wealth through conquest. When enough wealth has been accumulated, Greed gains ascendancy over Fear and produces the economic mind.

In the second main era of cultural evolution, which Adams calls Civilization, economic activities dominate, taking the form of plutocratic capitalism and the exploitation of society by the money-changers. Morale, racial virility, art and social institutions tend to decay as a result of this corrosive process, fathered by the bourgeoisie, and the net result is an inevitable return to Barbarism.

To illustrate his theory of history, Mr. Adams turned especially to the "fall" of Rome, the Protestant Reformation, and the British Empire. His theory of the dominant influence of money power led him to lay special stress upon the rule of the monetary exchanges in each of these epochs of history. The

tyranny of the usurer brought about the fall of Rome and reversion to medievalism, where the revived régime of Fear encouraged war and creative artistic achievements. The Reformation renewed the tendency towards centralization, with mankind becoming once more primarily concerned about economic
matters, promoted the growth of capitalism, and produced a
return to the dominion of Greed and the economic mind, which
had earlier doomed Rome. England, through the combined impact of the Reformation and imperial expansion, represented
the most extreme triumph of these centralizing and financial
tendencies which are, according to Mr. Adams, ultimately to
return society once more to Anarchy, Fear and Barbarism.

If we accept Mr. Adams' line of historical reasoning neither
world organization nor Utopia lies ahead of us. Rather, an
ominous prospect of cultural and institutional disintegration
lies in the offing. Indeed, the second World War may have hastened us in this direction with unprecedented speed. If this un-
happy destiny of the race is not inevitable, it is surely sufficiently possible to warrant our reckoning with its implications
and taking what steps we may to avert its realization.

We may agree with Charles Austin Beard that Adams' theory
of history is highly stimulating, if not always borne out by the
facts, though his emphasis upon the economic aspects of the
Reformation is in accord with later scholarship. If few take
seriously any longer the cyclical theory of history, it is also true
that discriminating students no longer accept the idea of inevitable, universal and unilateral progress.

Most historians today would reverse Adams' emphasis upon
the creative factors in history. Fear seems far more likely to
breed intolerance, stagnation, superstition and violence, than
notable cultural achievements. On the other hand, commerce is
regarded as one of the great civilizing agencies of history. The
expansion of Europe and the Commercial Revolution after 1450

are looked upon as the most dynamic forces in creating modern civilization, just as Periclean Athens was the product of temporary commercial dominion and prosperity. Capitalism has, assuredly, produced plenty of exploitation and waste, but Soviet Russia demonstrates that the destruction of capitalism may not produce a return to primitive barbarism. But perhaps the main weakness in Adams' approach to history is his relative neglect of the technological elements in human destiny. Our modern empire of machines renders the comparison of our age with any earlier period highly misleading in many respects.

II. OSWALD SPENGLER ON THE DECLINE OF WESTERN CULTURE

After Adams' *Law of Civilization and Decay,* the next survey of social evolution which aroused international interest was that made by Oswald Spengler, who shared Adams' pessimistic view of the nature and course of the history of mankind.

The notion that human history moves in ever-recurring cycles is an old one which dates back to Plato. The publication of Spengler's *Der Untergang des Abendlandes* (*The Decline of the West*), which appeared in two volumes in 1917, 1921, was the most influential contemporary revival of this doctrine. This voluminous work combined the cyclical theory of historical development, a wholehearted acceptance of the organismic theory of society and social evolution, and the Romanticist idea of a culture-soul which dominates the traits and activities of any people. Each great historic social unity constitutes what Spengler calls a Culture. Every culture is a self-contained organism that passes through a pre-ordained and inevitable life-cycle in response to the power of Destiny, which Spengler holds to be the guiding force in social evolution. He contends that the life-cycle of cultures is not subject to the ordinary laws of cause and effect.

History rises above the range of conventional causality. Each culture has an all-pervading culture-soul of which any people are a unit and their historic achievements a direct product. The interpretation of history becomes mainly a reading of the meaning and expression of the culture-soul, as judged by its products in the external events of history—what Spengler calls the "art of Physiognomic."

All great historic cultures pass through the inevitable stages of the life-cycle of any organism: birth, youth, maturity and old age, or, as Spengler sometimes expresses it in seasonal terms—spring, summer, autumn and winter. Each of these historic cultures experiences parallel or identical stages in its life-cycle, but these stages do not have identical forms of expression in historical achievements, for the various cultures have different culture-souls. Therefore, their products will be different, even though the general pattern and the sequence of the stages in the life-cycle are identical. Every main historic culture ends up by becoming a Civilization. Civilization is the terminal or decadent stage of cultures. It is the period when the culture-soul has lost all of its creative power. It is the epoch of old-age or winter for the culture: "Civilizations are the most external and artificial states of which a species of developing humanity is capable. They are a conclusion, the thing-become succeeding the thing-becoming, death following life, rigidity following expansion, intellectual age and the stone-built petrifying world-city following mother earth and the spiritual childhood of the Doric and Gothic. They are an end, irrevocable, yet by inward necessity reached again and again." [2]

Our western society passed from a culture to civilization during the course of the nineteenth century. The transition was characterized by the growth of great city (megalopolitan) populations, materialism, exploitation, scepticism, atheism, imperialism and war. Western civilization is henceforth doomed to war, Caesarism, base animal strivings, and ultimate extinction. There has been no significant interrelation between the main organic cultures of the past. Nothing can vitally alter the sequence or duration of the stages of their development or hasten or delay the manifestation of the dominant historic trends.

Passing from these grandiose generalities to something resembling the actual history of mankind, its institutions and culture, Spengler contends that there have been some six great historic cultures—the Egyptian, the Old Chinese, the Classical, the Indian, the Arabian and the Western. Conceived in terms of historical processes and events, rather than organismic poetry, each culture goes through the following stages of development in every case, whatever the differences in detail, due to individual and unique culture-souls.

First, there is what Spengler calls the Pre-Culture Era, which is characterized by tribal or gentile society, absence of the territorial state, and primitive superstition and symbolism. Next comes what he designates as the stage of Culture, which is divided into two periods. In the first or Early Culture period the territorial state and civic life come into existence. The earliest form of political organization is feudalism which rests on personal relations. This is soon supplanted by the aristocratic state which installs true civil society. In this period the rural economy and community are predominant, though towns and cities begin to make their appearance. Culture is rudimentary, for Spengler does not believe the peasantry capable of producing any high form of culture.

Gradually, there develops what Spengler calls the Late Culture Period. Society becomes overwhelmingly urban and life becomes mainly city life. A high culture now becomes possible, for Spengler holds that it is a conclusive fact that all great cultures are urban cultures. True world history is the history of city dwellers. The middle class, or bourgeoisie, overthrow the landed gentry, and capitalism and a money economy come to dominate economic life. Parliamentary government may arise to promote the political power of the bourgeoisie. It is a period in which art flourishes and intellectual creativity is at its height. Despite the fact that Spengler devotes unusual attention to what is generally known as cultural history, he holds that politics is the highest expression of human activity: "Politics in the highest sense is life and life is politics."

Though all high human culture is an urban culture, the progress of urbanization ultimately destroys creativity and leads to that degradation and decadence of life which Spengler calls Civilization. More and larger cities develop; the city becomes a megalopolis and urban life becomes megalopolitan and demoralizing. Intellectual and artistic creativity disappear. Megalopolitan life produces "the masses," crowds, mobs and democratic politics. The plutocracy exploit society, while the masses are venal and incompetent. Materialism and scepticism undermine social morale. Imperialism and war bring waste and ruin in their wake. Nervous tensions and new strains and stresses help along the process of decline and ultimate chaos. As we have pointed out, Spengler believes that our Western culture is already well advanced in the decadent period of civilization. It is doomed and without hope of rehabilitation. The next great historic culture may arise in the Far East.

In appraising Spengler's work, one may fairly say that his general theory of social evolution—his historical sociology—is essentially pure fancy, if not fantasy. His idea of a dominant culture-soul, and of the overwhelming power of Destiny, his denial of any causality in history, and the like, are akin to the views of the Romanticist philosophers of history of the late eighteenth and early nineteenth centuries. His notion of the life-cycle of cultures as stages of organic growth is a revival of the discarded organismic theory of society. The only semblance to historical reality in his work is his outline of the stages of institutional and cultural development, in which there is little originality save for what is arbitrary and questionable, such as his strange use of the term civilization. Then, there is much which is contradictory in his theories. While denying causality in history, he dogmatically utilizes the culture-soul and Destiny as the actual causes of historic experiences and mutations. Also, his assertion of parallel or identical stages in the life-cycle of each cultural organism implies a basic cause for this uniformity —the laws of organic development.

The main value of his work is that of a contribution to literary —or historical—aesthetics, a monumental example of historical poetry. Other items of some importance are his accumulation of a vast mass of facts, some of them reliable, and numerous brilliant surmises and interpretations which often possess some validity. At the time of the publication of his work Spengler's philosophy attained great popularity because of the general pessimism following the first World War. It's vogue may be revived as the crisis grows deeper following the second World War. And there may be some validity in Spengler's contention that the Western era is in its terminal stages—surely Western civilization has made frantic efforts to commit suicide since Spengler's day. But, whether Spengler's guesses turn out to be true or false, little can be said in favor of his method of approaching historical sociology.

III. ARNOLD J. TOYNBEE BURIES THE UNIVERSE IN AN ANGLICAN CHURCHYARD

The work on social evolution and the history of humanity which is currently receiving the greatest amount of discussion among Anglo-American readers is Arnold J. Toynbee's *A Study of History,* the popularity of which is enhanced by the conditions following the second World War, as Spengler's vogue was partly to be explained by the conditions at the end of the first World War.[3]

Toynbee published the first three volumes of *A Study of History*, in 1933. This initial installment was devoted primarily to a statement of the problem and the general principles to be followed, and to the genesis of some twenty-one selected civilizations. Three more volumes appeared in 1939. These were mainly taken up with a description of the decline and disintegration of these civilizations. Three more volumes are promised. Those to come are supposed to handle the problem of the contacts and rhythms in the development of historic civilizations, the outcome of Western civilization, the sources of inspiration for historians, and the lesson of all this for our age.

Taking as his unit of investigation the origin and destiny of specific civilizations, Toynbee finds that there have been some twenty-one altogether in the course of history, along with certain peripheral cultures which never attained a true civilization. He first lists nineteen such civilizations: the Egyptiac, Sumeric, Babylonic, Hittite, Syriac, Minoan, Hellenic, Iranic, Arabic, Hindu, Indic, Sinic, Far Eastern, Andean, Yucatec, Mayan, Mexic, Orthodox Christian, and Western. He gets his twenty-one by dividing the Orthodox Christian into Orthodox Byzantine and Orthodox Russian; and the Far Eastern into Chinese and Korean-Japanese.

During the course of recorded history, the "civilizational" process has disposed of all but seven of these world civilizations: the Orthodox Christian, the Orthodox Russian, the Islamic (which combines the Iranic and Arabic civilizations of the original list), the Hindu, the Chinese, the Korean-Japanese, and the Western (Western Europe, the British Commonwealth, the United States, and Latin America).

All of these seven except Western civilization are in their

terminal stages and have already fallen into the orbit of Western civilization. Their period of basic breakdown runs from 977 for Orthodox Christianity, to 1500 for Islamic civilization. Even the outcome for Western civilization is highly uncertain and it may turn out that its period of breakdown is to be located in the Conciliar Movement of the 15th century or the Religious Wars of the 16th.

The main assurance of salvation for Western civilization resides in two facts: (1) we have not yet reached the period of the "universal state" which always portends inevitable dissolution; and (2) we may have the good sense and inspiration to recognize the destiny for which God has intended us and rise to claim our divine heritage through Christ's Incarnation before it is too late. The chief hope for this second possibility lies in a great revival of Christian faith and zeal. In the case of every civilization, the period of actual breakdown comes prior to the era which is usually regarded as the height of that civilization; therefore, the "Golden Ages" of all civilizations are invariably periods of "Indian Summer."

We have space only for a very brief summary of the course of each civilization studied by Toynbee, the process being essentially the same in all cases. Civilization arises from what he calls challenge-and-response—which is roughly man's response to the challenge from the physical environment. In this process, leadership is maintained by what he calls a creative minority whom the masses follow willingly because of admiration and respect. But when civilization has been attained the creative minority inevitably lose their spiritual creativity and become transformed into what he designates as the dominant minority, thus bringing about the so-called "time of troubles" which takes the form of class struggles and parochial wars within the civilization, of external conflicts with other civilizations, and of schisms in the souls of the citizens. Some members of the creative minority who remain may seek relief in what Toynbee calls withdrawal-and-response, namely, retirement, communion with God, and the searching of their souls. As a result, they become "etherialized" and may regain some power of leadership, but so far this has never sufficed to solve the problems of the time of troubles. Saviors of various kinds arise, but there has been only one authentic savior, Jesus of Nazareth—"The King of the Kingdom of God." Christ's Incarnation is described as the central fact of all human history and the only hope of civilization.

The dominant minority seek to save the situation by creating a universal state to curb parochial wars within the civilization. To combat this, the discontented "internal proletariat" build up a universal church. In time, the dominant minority succumb and accept the universal church of the internal proletariat. In the meantime, an "external proletariat," namely, the barbarians at the gate, seek to intrude their manners and customs. Eventually, the dominant minority accept these also, and the civilization is then on the high road to disintegration, though it may have centuries of fictitious prosperity and glory before complete collapse takes place. Western civilization has little hope of survival except in a Second Coming of Our Lord under Anglican auspices.

As a critical appraisal of Toynbee's work we may say that, despite its title, it is not really a history at all, or a "study of history." It is, literally, as Howard Becker pointed out years ago, a "Theodicy," which the dictionary defines as a "vindication of divine justice in permitting evil to exist in the world"— in Toynbee's own terms, allowing man to move from the beatific passivity of the state of *Yin* into the ultimately doomed creative ordeal of the state of *Yang*. This is all interesting, but it is not objective, or even interpretative, *history*. It is theology employing selected facts of history to illustrate the will of God, as the medieval bestiaries utilized biological fantasies to achieve the same results. Toynbee's work differs from that of Orosius and Augustine chiefly in that he makes relatively more use of the deeds of men than of divine figures to prove much the same case. Toynbee's vast materials throw far more light upon the processes of Toynbee's mind than upon the actual processes of history.

As historical sociology, Toynbee's work has been hailed by some as a masterly contribution to what is called the "culture case study" method. Unfortunately, Toynbee had his "case" all made out before he studied it comparatively. He formulated his "case" in advance and then gave it plausibility by seeking and selecting comparable data from other "cases" to vindicate his original "case." The shortcomings of Toynbee as an exemplar of the culture case study method can best be comprehended by comparing his work in this respect with that of great masters in the field, such as Émile Durkheim and Max Weber.

Toynbee revives in sociology the erroneous method of the older evolutionary anthropologists who thought out in advance a pattern of cultural development and then sought ethnographic data rather promiscuously to confirm their theses. Toynbee built up a comparable scheme of human development. Spengler had written at length about the inevitable death of successive cultures through a loss of creative vitality. Winwood Reade had anticipated the notion of challenge-and-response. Toynbee's studies of Greek civilization had strongly suggested the rivalry of parochial states. His knowledge of the Roman Empire presented him with the fact of the creation of a universal state to curb the conflicts between parochial states within a civilization and with the panorama of the decline of a great universal society. Christianity provided a universal church. Rostovtzev had anticipated the idea of an internal and external proletariat. Toynbee wove all these notions into his theodicy and the result was the basic concepts of *A Study of History.* Then he combed materials on his twenty other civilizations to confirm his pattern of history and to elucidate his moral and theological conceptions. It is not unfair to say that he is more in error than evolutionary anthropologists like Lewis Henry Morgan, who held firmly and steadfastly to natural, evolutionary forces and did not invoke the hand of God in their behalf. Morgan is as far ahead of Toynbee here as Herbert Spencer's *First Principles* was of Augustine's *City of God*. If one wishes to get some notion of Toynbee's status as an historical sociologist, there would be no better exercise than to compare his book with Ralph Turner's *The Great Cultural Traditions,* and William Christie MacLeod's *Origin and History of Politics.*

IV. SOROKIN'S FLUCTUATING SOCIAL UNIVERSE

One of the most voluminous and remarkable contributions to historical sociology is the four-volume *Social and Cultural Dynamics* of Pitirim Sorokin (1889–   ), a Russian-born sociologist, resident in the United States since the Bolshevik Revolution of 1917.[4] In this work Sorokin proceeds to study the cultural trends in Western civilization since the early Greek period, with a number of excursions into oriental history. Three volumes appeared in 1937 and a fourth in 1941. The book assumes to be based upon a thorough application of the comparative method, buttressed by statistics. Yet it must be said that, because of the highly subjective character of Sorokin's categories and types and the application of the statistical method to non-quantitative materials, it is one of the most amazing distortions of scientific procedure in historical sociology which have thus far appeared. The book constantly compares the incomparable—such as comparing families and symphonies and widely variant periods of history and culture—and repeatedly seeks to measure the immeasurable.

Sorokin repudiates the idea of unilateral, or even any real, progress in civilization, as well as the notion of cycles of development, such as those postulated by Oswald Spengler. He finds only *fluctuations* from age to age—fluctuations which will never cease so long as the human race and culture persist. His book presents the fluctuations in art, philosophy, ethics, law and social institutions, including an elaborate analysis and comparison of wars and revolutions. The vast amount of historical material assembled is gathered less for the purpose of understanding history than to permit Sorokin to grade and evaluate his materials according to his subjective postulates and categories.

All societies and cultural traits are graded into two types: (1) the good or *ideational,* by which he means primarily those which are spiritual and based on faith; and (2) the bad or *sensate*—the secular, empirical and hedonistic. Rarely, a compromise is worked out between these two types. This compromise Sorokin designates as *idealistic.* The only periods in which the dominant trends in culture have been idealistic have been in fifth century Greece and in Western Europe during the thirteenth and fourteenth centuries.

In the course of his work, Sorokin outlines the main fluctuations which he alleges to have taken place in the dominant trends of civilization since the sixth century B.C. Down to the sixth century B.C., Greek culture was primarily ideational. Then sensate trends grew stronger and the result was the compromise that produced the idealistic Hellenic civilization of the fifth and early fourth centuries. From the fourth century B.C. to the third century A.D. Greco-Roman culture was predominantly sensate. With the triumph of Christianity, ideational trends prospered and culture then became primarily ideational until the end of the twelfth century. Once more, sensate trends became prominent and the culture of the thirteenth and fourteenth centuries was again an idealistic compromise. Beginning with the fifteenth century, the growth of science, technology, industrialism and secularism has resulted in the complete triumph of sensate trends and patterns of culture.

The sorry state of world affairs today represents the final crisis of this era of sensate dominance. As the breakdown approaches, ideational trends are becoming more numerous and powerful and an idealistic renaissance or compromise will take place. This may run its course and lead to a new ideational era which can last for centuries. But we may expect new sensate trends to arise in time and produce another sensate era.

The future thus offers us only the prospect of an endless series of fluctuations—ideational, sensate and idealistic eras. As Hans Speir has well put it: "In short, there is no final doomsday, there is only a condition, a prophecy of recurring doomsdays alternating with recurring days of a more fortunate lot of man." Sorokin thus gets rather close to the cyclical theory of history which he formally repudiates—cycles of endlessly recurring fluctuations of dominant cultural trends. Sorokin published a popular summary of his *Social and Cultural Dynamics* under the title of *The Crisis of Our Age* (1941).

Viewed as a method of studying the history of human society and culture, the author of this book is unable to take Sorokin's voluminous treatise at all seriously, save for the patient assembling of a vast array of what are at times valuable and interesting data. The whole work is more a product of Sorokin's mind than a record of the actual doings of mankind or a faithful review of the trends in social evolution. Quite as much as is the case with Toynbee's *A Study of History*, the book is more a revelation of the processes of the author's mind than of the course of human history. Again, like Toynbee's book, its methodological and mental affinity lies more with the philosophy of history which flourished from Herder to Hegel than with contemporary social science. If one shares Sorokin's subjective prejudices and biases, he will esteem his work. If he dislikes them, he will probably repudiate the book. But in either case the reaction is not likely to bear much relation to the actuality of history or the validity of Sorokin's materials and generalizations.

V. KARL LAMPRECHT AND CULTURAL HISTORY

While social and cultural history (*Kulturgeschichte*) is not historical sociology, it is closely related to it and furnishes indispensable material for the historical sociologist. Hence, some reference to it must be made in any survey of the development of historical sociology.[5]

The most aggressive champion of *Kulturgeschichte* and the most discussed person in connection with its development in contemporary times was Karl Lamprecht of Leipzig (1856–1910). Lamprecht's first important work was a long and original treatise on the economic history of medieval Germany, with special attention to the Moselle area. Here he indicated his interest in the history of economic groups and economic mass movements as affecting the social history of a people. This attitude he obtained in part from Karl Marx, though Lamprecht was not an orthodox Marxian. He was also much influenced by Comte's suggestion that history should be viewed as successive stages in the collective psychology of humanity, and he was deeply impressed by the doctrine of evolution.

From the time of the publication of the first volume of his classic *German History,* in 1891, until his death, Lamprecht accompanied his systematic historical work by an unending controversy with the exponents of the older historical notions. In this debate he upheld his thesis that "history is a sociopsychological science" concerned primarily with "sociopsychic" materials, as contrasted with the "individual-psychic" factors which had been emphasized by the previous conventional narrative and biographical history. To Lamprecht, history is the collective psychology of the past rather than collective biography, as had been the opinion of the typical historians who had generally followed Carlyle's views on historical causation, provided they paid any attention whatever to the problem of historical causation.

Working from the above premises, Lamprecht outlined what he regarded as the great stages in the sociopsychological development of Western civilization. The earliest or the primitive stage he designated as the "symbolic." This was superseded in the early Middle Ages by the "typical," that period of differentiation which produced various distinct types of culture. The later medieval period was the age of the "conventional" in culture, social life, industry, art, and religion. This was followed by the period of "individualism" from the Renaissance through the *Aufklärung.* This epoch in which, in the Protestant portions of Europe, the individual might hold direct communion with God, was everywhere distinguished by great individual works of genius in science, art, literature, commerce, and politics. Beginning with the Romanticists, and extending to the Industrial Revolution came the period of "subjectivism," characterized by a deep emotional revolt against rationalism. The period since the Industrial Revolution is declared to be one of "nervous tension" in which mankind is still groping for a central ideal or an organizing socio-psychic principle.

Though these stages or epochs provided the pattern for the organization of his voluminous *German History,* Lamprecht maintained that they are typical of social evolution in general among all peoples that have developed to the level of modern civilization.

Lamprecht did not ignore political history, but he subordinated it to economic and cultural history. His interest in economic history led him to lay special stress on economic factors in German development, and he also gave unusual attention to the history of art and music. Not only did Lamprecht write voluminously; he was also an eager and effective controversialist and did much to promote his views on history. He had considerable influence on Paul Lacombe and Henri Berr in France, Guglielmo Ferrero and Corado Barbagallo in Italy, Henri Pirenne in Belgium, and W. E. Dodd and Carl Becker in the United States.

While Lamprecht did not found a formal school in Germany, he left a strong influence. In 1909 his admirers enabled him to found the *Institut für Kultur-und-Universalgeschichte* at Leipzig to carry on the training of scholars in his tradition. A number of his disciples have done important work. Kurt Breysig, in his *Cultural History of Modern Times* (1901) applied Lamprecht's general ideas to a systematic survey of the cultural evolution of the modern world. Breysig's work is even more rigorously schematized and generalized than Lamprecht's, thus coming closer to historical sociology. In later years, Breysig devoted himself to intellectual history and the philosophy of history in his *On Historical Becoming* (1928).

VI. PAUL BARTH: SOCIOLOGY AS THE PHILOSOPHY OF HISTORY

The most ambitious and prolific efforts to produce large-scale interpretations of human society had been made in the pre-sociological era by the Romanticist philosophers of history, such as Herder, Fichte, Hegel, Schelling, Krause, Jouffroy, Quinet, Laurent, and others. We have already pointed out that Brooks Adams, Spengler, Toynbee and Sorokin have written more in the tradition of the subjective philosophy of history than in accord with strictly scientific sociology. It remained for a German historian and sociologist, Paul Barth (1858–1922), to try to combine the sweep and breadth of the older philosophy of history with the scientific tenets of contemporary sociology. This he did in his *Die Philosophie der Geschichte als Soziologie,* which first appeared in 1897 and was enlarged in subsequent editions, the last of which, the 4th, appeared in the year of Barth's death.[6]

Barth was a student of the older philosophy of history, especially of Hegel's version. He was impressed with the break which had developed between the scientific individualistic historiography of Leopold von Ranke, the philosophy of history, and Marxian historical dialectic. He hoped to restore a sound synthesis of these by retaining the breadth of view of the philosophy of history and its interest in the sequences of institutional development, while divesting it of its subjectivism and grandiose assumptions by founding it upon scientific principles. Barth believed that it is the function of sociology to produce this new synthesis. Sociology could be based upon the laws and methods of natural science and its subject-matter would be mainly the interpretation of the history of human society; in other words, the new and sounder philosophy of history. In short, sociology is a philosophy of history grounded firmly in scientific methodology. As a student of Wundt, Barth held that scientific psychology could render indispensable aid to sociology in interpreting history. A somewhat similar attitude to that of Barth was taken by Ludwig Stein (1859–1930) in his *Die Soziale Frage im Lichte der Philosophie* (1923), but Stein did not argue the point in any such elaborate theoretical and methodological fashion as did Barth, whose book constitutes perhaps the most extended and powerful argument ever set forth for the reality, logic and services of historical sociology.

VII. HERBERT GEORGE WELLS: HISTORICAL PROPAGANDA FOR THE WORLD STATE

No sketch of large-scale reviews of the historic experience of mankind would be complete without some reference to the vastly popular two-volume work of H. G. Wells, *The Outline of History,* which appeared in 1920 and was the most widely-read book of the post-war era.

In relation to historical sociology, the book was especially notable for its magnificent portrayal of the geological background of human history and the proper time perspective for a realistic appraisal thereof. Gratifying also was Wells' effort to present the civilizations of the East as well as the West. The second volume was, however, little more than an epitome of conventional history, with emphasis on the evils of war and the blessings of peace.

Wells contended that all history since the Cro-Magnon Man of some 25,000 years, or more, ago is fundamentally a history of ideas, there having been no biological progress in mankind during this period. Here is where history plays its rôle in promoting peace: "There can be no common peace and prosperity without common historical ideas. . . . A sense of history as the common adventure of all mankind is as necessary for peace within as it is for peace between nations." Wells died a disillusioned man, but his forthright rationalism and intellectual integrity stand out in shining contrast to the mystical fog currently being spread by his compatriot, Professor Toynbee.

---

1. Beard, *loc. cit.*
2. Spengler, *op. cit.* (New York: Knopf, 1926) Vol. I, p. 31; *Cf.* J. T. Shotwell, "Spengler: a Poetic Interpreter of History," *Current History,* May, 1929, pp. 283–287; and F. N. House, *The Range of Social Theory* (New York: Holt, 1929), pp. 377–382.
3. Barnes *et al., op. cit.,* Chap. XXXVII.
4. *Ibid.,* Chap. XLVI.
5. Barnes and Becker, *Contemporary Social Theory,* Chap. 16.
6. A. W. Small, *General Sociology* (Chicago: University of Chicago Press, 1905), pp. 44 ff.

CHAPTER VIII

SOCIOLOGICAL CONTRIBUTIONS TO AN UNDERSTANDING OF PERIODS OF CULTURE AND SPECIFIC INSTITUTIONS

I. PRIMITIVE LIFE AND INSTITUTIONS

While the greater part of the material bearing upon primitive social life and institutions has been produced by anthropologists, a number of sociologists have also contributed to this field. Several have outlined methods of studying primitive and historic cultures. We have already made mention of such writers. Steinmetz worked out a sociological science of primitive culture which he called sociography and for which he recommended a considerable use of the statistical method, as also did Hobhouse and Mazzarella. Ellwood, Chapin, Ogburn, Willey, Folsom, and Wallis, influenced by such anthropologists as Marett and the Boas school, have described the laws and processes of cultural development.

The great majority of the sociological contributions to the description and analysis of primitive life and society have been referred to in one way or another in earlier pages. Some sociologists have dealt broadly with primitive society. Examples are Vierkandt's comparative study of primitive and civilized peoples; the Sumner-Keller *Science of Society,* which deals in part with primitive customs and institutions; Thomas' two masterly volumes, *Source Book for Social Origins,* and *Primitive Behavior;* and Richard Thurnwald's great five-volume work, *Die Menschliche Gesellschaft in ihren ethno-soziologischen Grundlagen* (1930). Thurnwald's treatise is definitely the outstanding sociological contribution to the study of primitive society since Morgan's *Ancient Society,* and it is far more voluminous and more truly up-to-date and scientific than Morgan's pioneer work. Thurnwald systematically differentiates and describes the chief types of primitive societies, giving a well-rounded picture of their life, culture and institutions, along with the general socio-logical principles which they illustrate. Thurnwald thus stands at the head of present-day sociological students of primitive society.[1] He rejected classical evolutionism, as well as other one-sided interpretations of primitive culture and revealed a thor-ough knowledge of contemporary critical anthropology. In his interpretation of cultural and institutional development he aligned himself with the moderate functionalists.

Sociologists have also made special studies of primitive cul-ture, either of special phases thereof or of particular areas. MacLeod has dealt with primitive politics; Sumner with the mores and folkways; Durkheim, Webster, and Wallis with primitive religion; and Westermarck and Howard with primi-tive matrimonial institutions, customs, and ceremonials. Mac-Leod, in his *American Indian Frontier* (1928), has provided a good synthesis of American Indian life and of Indian contact with the whites; Durkheim, Hobhouse, Wheeler and Ginsberg dealt with Australian primitives; Westermarck investigated the natives of Morocco; Kovalevsky studied vestiges of primitive customs and institutions among the inhabitants of the Caucasus; and Thurnwald did important work on the former German islands in the Pacific.

II. ANCIENT AND MEDIEVAL TIMES

Sociologists have made important contributions to our knowl-edge of social evolution in ancient times. Max Weber carried out epoch-making studies of the early agricultural civilizations, of Jewish life and ceremonials, and of the interrelation of religion, rationalism and economic life in China and India. Especially notable was Weber's *Die römische Agrargeschichte in ihrer Bedeutung für das Staats-und-Privatrecht* (1891). Alfred Weber offered important contributions to the study of the development and changes in Egyptian civilization. Franz Oppenheimer devoted much attention to economic life in early civilizations with special reference to the rise of land monopoly. Howard Becker has dealt with the growth of secularization in Hellenic society. Toynbee's formula for organizing the data about the rise, development and decline of civilizations was derived from his initial study of Hellenic civilization, and his account of Hellenic civilization is the most reliable portion of his *A Study of History,* though he minimizes the effect of rational and material factors. Teggart made an interesting comparative study of war and uprisings in Rome and China from 58 B.C. to 107 A.D. in his *Rome and China* (1939).

Lippert and Troeltsch made important contributions to the rise of Christianity, and Sorokin devoted considerable space to medieval civilization in his analysis of the fluctuations of ideational, idealistic, and sensate cultures during this era. Kovalevsky's classic work on the economic history of Europe gave elaborate attention to medieval economic history. Some of the most scholarly phases of Kovalevsky's work were concentrated on the transition from medieval to early modern society, especially in the case of England. He also contributed much to our knowledge of the evolution of economic society in early modern times.

III. THE RISE OF PROTESTANTISM AND CAPITALISM

Sociologists have done much to extend and clarify our information on the origins of modern society, especially with respect to the rise of capitalism and Protestantism and the interrelation between religion and economics in early modern times. Werner Sombart (1863–1941) gave us the definitive study of the evolution of capitalism in his great work, *Der moderne Kapitalismus,* first published in 1902, and issued in a later and expanded edition between 1916 and 1927.[2] He wrote a number of other books dealing with special phases of the origins and manifestation of capitalism.

Sombart envisaged capitalism as a socio-economic system based on exchange and motivated by the spirit of unlimited acquisition. The profit motive is predominant in capitalism and it was facilitated by the rise of double-entry bookkeeping, which made possible an accurate accounting of profit and loss, and by the depersonalization of economic activities and relationships. Sociologically speaking, the essence of capitalism is "the institutionalization of self-interest." Capitalism developed slowly, and it was not until about 1760 that the era of what Sombart calls "high" or completely developed capitalism emerged in Western society. It endured as the dominant economic system of the Western world down to the outbreak of the second World War.

Sombart had laid great stress on the vital rôle of the "spirit" of capitalism but he failed to make it clear how this acquisitive spirit first emerged in early modern times. The answer was supplied by Max Weber in one of the most illuminating and much-controverted contributions ever made to historical sociology, his *Protestant Ethic and the Spirit of Capitalism,* published in 1905, and followed the next year by his *The Protestant Sects and the Spirit of Capitalism.*[3] Luther had designated business as a "calling" (*Beruf*), and Calvin gave it an acquisitive cast by linking spiritual salvation with business success. Prosperity in business was regarded as a sign of spiritual grace. Hard work and thrift were commendable phases of this-worldly asceticism. The dynamic acquisitive spirit of capitalism which Protestantism supplied endured after society had become partly secularized and the original religious background had melted away. Capitalism and its spirit in time became institutionalized in a series of bureaucratic structures. Weber did not contend that Protestantism, especially Calvinism, was the sole cause of capitalism, which he regarded as having been produced by many factors, but he did hold that, without the Protestant ethics, capitalism would not have made its appearance. Efforts to discredit Weber's thesis by H. M. Robertson and others have failed signally.

Weber's interest in Protestantism was incidental to his concern with economic and social history and institutional development. In the case of Ernst Troeltsch (1865–1923) the interest was primarily in the religious import of Protestantism, though he dealt in a discriminating fashion with the relation of Protestantism to the rise of capitalism.[4] Troeltsch's books represent, perhaps, the most impressive sociological study of the history of Christianity down to contemporary times. His most important writings were *Die Bedeutung des Protestantismus für die Entstehung der modernen Welt* (1906; translated as *Protestantism and Progress*); and *Die Soziallehren der christlichen Kirchen und Gruppen* (2 vols., 1912; translated as *The Social Teachings of the Christian Churches*).

Troeltsch regarded primitive Christianity as a predominantly spiritual movement based on the idea of the equality of all before God. But during the Middle Ages it succumbed to institutionalism and tradition; whatever spiritual and dynamic impulses survived were centered mainly in the monasteries. Protestantism, in its origins, was neither a creature of modern times nor did it produce modern society. It was, originally, primarily a reversion to medievalism. But, incidentally and indirectly, it stimulated modern tendencies, such as the origins of religious liberty, the rise of nationalism, the growth of the middle class, and the development of capitalism. Troeltsch made an important distinction between churches, which he regarded as continuing the unifying and institutionalizing rôle of the medieval Church, and sects, which he held to be radically inclined and supported mainly by the lower classes.

In a broad way, Troeltsch agreed with Max Weber that Protestantism contributed powerfully to the growth of capitalism. But he did not support Weber's contention that Protestantism had inspired and created the spirit of capitalism; rather, he held that it favored and fostered a capitalism which arose from many other factors. But, after all is said and done, Protestantism, according to Troeltsch, was chiefly important for its own intrinsic religious impulses and spirit rather than for its aid to other and secular tendencies and institutions.

The views of Troeltsch on the relation of Protestantism to capitalism were shared by the famous Munich sociologist and economic historian, Professor Lujo Brentano, whose ideas on the subject are best brought together in his *Der Wirtschaftende Mensch in der Geschichte* (1923). Many authorities regard this book as the sanest and most competent of all accounts of the nature and rise of capitalism. It will be apparent that Brentano differed widely in certain ways from both Sombart and Weber.

Brentano holds that the essentials of capitalism are the motive of rationalistic gain-seeking combined with freedom of contract. He contends that the gain-seeking motive has been present in all periods of recorded history among certain classes. It was simply relatively submerged in ancient and medieval times because of the ascendancy of philosophical, ethical and religious systems and interests which were primarily devoted to other ends and aims than gain-seeking. But even then it was present in such cases as the Roman *publicani,* business men and merchants—even in the economic motivation of monastic industry.

Capitalism began to get under way in full momentum with

the rise of the Italian commercial cities at the close of the Middle Ages and was greatly stimulated by the expansion of Europe, the Commercial Revolution, and the development of Mercantilism. It did not owe its origin to Protestantism. Protestant ethics only helped to popularize and diffuse the spirit and methods of capitalism. The moral value of work is an old idea, and Christian medieval philosophy stressed the moral obligation to follow one's economic vocation. Protestantism thus served to complete the establishment of capitalism as the dominant economic institution of modern times rather than bringing it into existence or being indispensable to its origin. Brentano also gained fame as an historian of labor organization, being noted for his defense of the generally rejected notion that our labor unions are directly descended from the medieval guilds, a view successfully refuted by the Webbs and other economic historians.

The outstanding American student of the evolution of capitalism was Thorstein Bunde Veblen (1857–1929).[5] Veblen is usually listed as an economist but his studies of the modern economic order were based more upon sociology and social psychology than upon traditional economics, which he regarded as no more than a rationalization and apology for the existing economic system of capitalism. Whereas Sombart had stressed acquisition as the chief trait of capitalism, Veblen extended this conception so far as to imply that capitalism is predominantly predatory, as well as acquisitive. He showed how the pirate captain has evolved into the captain of industry and the robber baron into the financial magnate. He regarded the increasing profits of enterprise as chiefly due to an improving technology of abundance rather than to any economic statesmanship on the part of the rulers of industry. This idea made Veblen popular with the advocates of Technocracy. He laid special stress upon absentee ownership and the separation of ownership from management as the dominant means and technique of predatory exploitation in our period of what Sombart had called "high capitalism." With withering irony and caustic humor, Veblen described in his *The Theory of the Leisure Class* (1899) the behavior traits which the capitalist class has built up for itself, such as conspicuous waste and honorific consumption, ostentatious abstention from labor, and the like. He also stressed the reaction of capitalist psychology on education in his *The Higher Learning in America* (1919). Other important books were his *The Theory of Business Enterprise* (1904); *The Instinct of Workmanship* (1914); *The Engineers and the Price System* (1921); and *Absentee Ownership* (1923).

Albion W. Small (1854–1926) was sympathetic with Veblen, but he laid more stress on the conflict of social classes that came as a result of the rise of capitalism. This idea he embodied in his *Between Eras: from Capitalism to Democracy* (1913), but he developed this theme more completely in his famous university lectures on the subject. Small did more than anybody else of his era to introduce into American thought the Germanic sociological literature on capitalism as expressed by Sombart, Weber, Troeltsch, Schmoller, Wagner, and others.[6]

IV. RISE OF REPRESENTATIVE GOVERNMENT AND DEMOCRACY

If capitalism was the most important economic development in modern times, the rise of parliamentary government, and later of democracy, was one of the two chief political innovations of the modern age. The outstanding sociological contribution to the origins of representative government were made in the voluminous works of Kovalevsky, who wrote a four-volume book on *The Origin of Modern Democracy* (1897), and three volumes on *From Direct to Representative Democracy and From Patriarchal Monarchy to Parliamentarianism* (1906).[7]

He traced the development of legal equality and popular sovereignty, the achievements of the Levellers in England, and the reforms of the French Revolution. While conceding the importance of economic and social factors, especially the rise of commerce and industrialism and population growth, in the triumph of representative government and democracy, Kovalevsky also emphasized the power of liberal ideas and the influence of the polemical tracts issued in behalf of parliamentarianism, democracy, and liberty. Another valiant sociological defender of democracy was Hobhouse, who dealt with the subject in many books, but especially in his *Liberalism* (1912) and *Democracy and Reaction* (1905).[8] In the latter, Hobhouse stressed the extent and manner in which colonialism and imperialism impeded and burdened democracy. In this attitude he was heartily joined—even anticipated—by William Graham Sumner. Benjamin Kidd, in his *Control of the Tropics* (1898), and Giddings, in his *Democracy and Empire* (1900), on the other hand, sought to bring sociological principles to the support of imperialism. While an opponent of imperialism, Small laid more stress upon the economic corruption, inequalities and injustices arising out of capitalism as obstacles to the realization of any true democracy.

V. NATIONALISM AND TOTALITARIANISM

A number of sociologists traced the evolution of the national state and the spirit of nationalism. Such were Gumplowicz; the Dutch sociologist, S. R. Steinmetz; the German sociologists, Oppenheimer, Vierkandt, Paul Barth and Hans Fryer; the Italian-Swiss sociologist, Robert Michels; the French sociologists, Alfred Fouillée and Gustave Le Bon; and the Italian sociologist, Scipio Sighele. Jacques Novicow deplored extreme nationalistic developments and devoted several books to the defense of federalism and internationalism as the next stage in political evolution. Among the sociologists who, after the first World War, defended the idea of internationalism and the League of Nations probably the first place would have to be assigned to Hobhouse and Ludwig Stein.

The majority of sociologists in recent times remained true to their traditional defense of liberalism and democracy. But a number either stimulated totalitarian ideas or actually went over to the totalitarian camp.[9] The Italian sociologists, Gaetano Mosca and Vilfredo Pareto, laid great stress on the predominant rôle of the élite in political society, which was seized upon by the Fascists in their ideas of the "leadership" principle and the rule of the élite. The German sociologist, Hans Fryer (1887–), while never openly aligning himself with the National Socialists, defended authoritarianism, the rule of the élite, and national planning in his *Revolution von Rechts* (1931), *Herrschaft und Planung* (1933), and *Das politische Semester* (1933). Sombart definitely went over to National Socialism and defended his position in his *Deutscher Sozialmus* (1934, translated as *A New Social Philosophy,* 1937).

VI. CONTEMPORARY PROBLEMS AND WORLD CRISIS

When we come to more or less strictly contemporary culture and institutions the great majority of the research and writing has been done by sociologists of one type or another, but especially by those interested in some aspect of human welfare. There are a number of reasons for this. Many historians cling to the traditional idea that the historian can deal accurately only with material relatively remote from the present day. Those historians who presume to treat of contemporary times usually give us mainly narratives and description rather than an analysis of culture and institutions. Economists, political scientists and legalists very often treat mainly of theory, and if they do analyze institutions they have a rather narrow and specialized interest and range of operations.

Probably the most important contribution of sociologists to the understanding of modern social problems has been to envisage them as the product of cultural lag, or the failure of our social thinking and institutions to keep pace with the progress of science and technology—our material culture. The extent to which sociologists have dominated the field of contemporary culture and institutions can be readily discerned by consulting such representative biblographies of books on contemporary society as those contained in the writer's *Society in Transition,* and *Social Institutions.*

In promoting the scientific sociological study of contemporary social problems it is probable that the most important methodological contribution was made by W. I. Thomas and Florian Znaniecki in what is known as the life-history and personal documentation approach. They developed this in the long Methodological Note to *The Polish Peasant,* and Znaniecki elaborated it in his *The Method of Sociology* (1934). They also made an important contribution to the study of social pathology and maladjustment by regarding such social problems as a manifestation of the process of "social disorganization."

VII. THE EVOLUTION OF SOCIAL INSTITUTIONS

One of the more notable and substantial of the sociological contributions to historical sociology resides in the studies which sociologists have made of the origin and development of the leading social institutions. Sumner, Keller, Müller-Lyer, L. V. Ballard, J. O. Hertzler, and Constantine Panunzio have written on the origin and nature of social institutions in general. Important studies of the origin, nature, and social processes in the state have been made by such sociologists as Gumplowicz, Ratzenhofer, Oppenheimer, Small, Bentley, Graham Wallas, and McLeod. Gumplowicz and Tarde are justly famed for their work on the history and nature of law. Even more important has been the impact of the sociological approach to law on such students of jurisprudence as Gierke, Kantorowicz, Berolzheimer, Duguit, Maitland, Holmes and Pound. We have reviewed the work of Oppenheimer, Sombart, Max Weber, Veblen and Small on economic institutions. Tarde's *Psychologie économique* (1902) was an important contribution to realistic, institutional economics. The institution of property has been studied effectively by Hobhouse and by Ernest Beaglehole (*Property: A Study in Social Psychology,* 1931). The books on the family by Westermarck, Howard, Calhoun, Müller-Lyer, and Waller are sociological classics. Tönnies and R. M. MacIver have dealt with the sociological basis of the community. Durkheim, Hobhouse, Webster, Ellwood and Wallis have treated the evolution and social significance of religion. The sociological rôle and services of education have been handled in most fundamental fashion by Ward, Durkheim, Wallas, Giddings and George S. Counts. Such sociologists as George A. Lundberg, Henry Pratt Fairchild and Floyd H. Allport have devoted attention to the problem of recreation and the use of leisure time, which will become an ever more important social issue, provided we do not wipe out all civilization through mechanized warfare and atomic bombing. War as a social institution has received special attention from Maurice R. Davie, L. L. Bernard and Steinmetz. Revolution as a method of achieving institutional changes has been treated at length by Ellwood, Sorokin and LeBon. These writers have made it clear that, invariably, revolutions are not produced by radicals but by reactionaries who obstruct and frustrate gradual and orderly changes in society.

1. Lowie, *History of Ethnological Theory*, pp. 242–249.
2. Barnes *et al.*, *op. cit.*, Chap. XV.
3. *Ibid.*, Chap. XIII.
4. *Ibid.*, Chap. XIV.
5. Joseph Dorfman, *Thorstein Veblen and His America* (New York: Viking Press, 1934).
6. Barnes *et al.*, *op. cit.*, Chap. XXXIX.
7. *Ibid.*, Chap. XXIII.
8. *Ibid.*, Chap. XXXII.
9. *Ibid.*, Chaps. XVIII, XXIX.

CHAPTER IX

THE RELATIVE DECLINE OF INTEREST IN HISTORI-
CAL SOCIOLOGY IN THE TWENTIETH CENTURY

Perhaps the most striking aspect of the history of historical sociology is the decline in the interest in this field in the last four decades. From Comte to Giddings the historical aspects of society and social problems interested more sociological writers than any other phase of the subject. Even many comprehensive works on the "principles of sociology" devoted more attention to social evolution than to the analysis of other sociological data. In the twentieth century, however, there has been a marked decline of interest in historical sociology. After the publication of Giddings' *Principles of Sociology* in 1896 there had not been a single systematic treatment of the history of human society produced in this country until the appearance of Chapin's *Introduction to Social Evolution* in 1913, and his *Historical Introduction to Social Economy* in 1917, and of E. C. Hayes' textbook on sociology in 1915. There does not exist today in any language even one monumental and complete book on the history of human society—a synthesis of social evolution. Even the works on special aspects of historical sociology, such as Hobhouse's *Morals in Evolution,* Oppenheimer's *The State,* Westermarck's *Origin and Development of the Moral Ideas,* Sombart's history of capitalism, and Max Weber's comparative studies on religion and economics, have been few, indeed, compared with the vast output in the fields of analytical, biological, psychological, statistical, and, above all, applied, sociology. The recent comprehensive works on historical sociology by Spengler,

Toynbee and Sorokin have been motivated chiefly by subjective and emotional convictions rather than by the desire to trace social evolution in any literal and realistic fashion, thus standing closer to the old philosophy of history than to historical sociology.

It is not easy to discover a complete explanation for this falling-off of interest in historical sociology, but it seems safe to assert that it has been primarily due to the rise of activity in other fields through which an approach might be made to sociological problems. The historical and the biological methods were in the air between 1850 and 1900, and it was but natural that they should come to influence greatly, if not to dominate, the sociological works of this period. At the close of the century the analytical, psychological, and statistical methods of investigating sociological problems were just becoming popular, and it is not surprising that these methods should come to usurp the sociological field for a generation with most fertile and valuable results. The growth of state activity in this period, the reaction of sociology upon charity and philanthropy, and the greater pecuniary advantages of specialization in applied or practical sociology, served to give this field a popularity which quite exceeded that of any other.

Another influence which unquestionably operated indirectly to diminish the activity and interest in the field of historical sociology was the rise of social history in the writings of such historians as Green, Blok, Rambaud, Lamprecht, Breysig, Steinhausen, Turner, Thompson and Beard. Historians of this type remedied in part the shortcomings of historical sociology in recent years. In fact, the social historians and the anthropologists were about the only scholars who kept alive an active interest in social genesis. Sociologists were often inclined to look for historical data in the works of the social historians instead of gathering it themselves, and were not averse to shifting the burden of investigating social origins to the anthropologists.

This collapse of historical sociology after 1900 was doubly dasastrous, for it was during just this time that the critical anthropologists, the scientific advocates of culture case-study in sociology, and the well-trained social historians were putting in the hands of the sociologists a new and more reliable technique for exploring the history of human society. The older historical sociology had been built up on the doubtful foundations of social Darwinism and comparative anthropology, but, by the time that the newer critical anthropology appeared, there was little or no historical sociology to take advantage of its revolutionary achieved results. Yet, this should now prove an added impetus to the revival of the historical approach to sociological problems, for today we have unprecedented assurance that the execution of careful work in this field according to the newer methods will yield significant results of a permanently valuable character. The efforts of White and others to revive evolutionism on a sound factual basis as a science of culturology are especially significant and promising. This may provide the framework and principles for a valid methodology in socio-evolutionary studies.

A sound and reliable historical sociology, giving us an accurate account of the development of human society and its institutions, would have a value far beyond yielding pedantic satisfaction. Such knowledge is one of the indispensable preliminaries to any valid scheme or program for social reform, as well as one of the most potent forces likely to generate a desire for social improvement. As Professor James Harvey Robinson very succinctly and cogently expressed this thought:

Society is today engaged in a tremendous and unprecedented effort to better itself in manifold ways. Never has our knowledge of the world and of man been so great as it is now; never before has there been so much general good will and so much intelligent social activity as now prevails. The part that each of us can play in forwarding some phase of this reform will depend upon our understanding of existing conditions and opinion, and these can only be explained, as has been shown, by following more or less carefully the processes that produced them. We must develop historical-mindedness upon a far more generous scale than hitherto, for this will add a still deficient element in our intellectual equipment and will promote rational progress as nothing else can do. The present has hitherto been the willing victim of the past; the time has now come when it should turn on the past and exploit it in the interests of advance.[1]

It may be safely contended that, however much aid they may obtain from anthropologists and historians, the sociologists cannot afford to allow their historical viewpoint and information to be developed for them by any other group of students. No other than a sociologist with a genetic point of view and a command of accurate historical methodology will be likely to have that broad synthetic approach to the study of social development which is the great desideratum of contemporary social science.

And only a trained sociologist can reliably elucidate the illuminating sociological principles involved in social evolution. We must rely upon sociologists to apply sociological principles both in working out systematic treatises on social evolution and in drawing the more fruitful sociological conclusions from such studies.

---

1. *The New History* (New York: Macmillan, 1912), pp. 23–24.

PART III

Some Practical Applications of Historical Sociology

CHAPTER X

WORLD REVOLUTION, CULTURAL LAG, AND THE OUTLOOK FOR THE FUTURE

I. WE ARE IN THE MIDST OF THE FOURTH GREAT WORLD REVOLUTION IN HUMAN EXPERIENCE

In the preceding pages we have traced the development of historical sociology and its contribution to our knowledge of the evolution of human society. In the pages to follow we shall indicate some of the practical applications of historical sociology to current social problems and the solution of our world crisis. These contributions are primarily three in number: (1) the history of our leading social institutions; (2) the relation of cultural lag or institutional maladjustment to our present complex of social problems and the current world crisis; and (3) a critique of the theory of progress in the light of the facts of social evolution. The first of these is, obviously, far too extensive to be treated here. I have dealt with it at length in my work on *Social Institutions* (1942). We shall limit ourselves to a consideration of cultural lag and the theory of progress.

Far and away the most illuminating and vital aspect of contemporary social experience is its general setting in the world trends of our time—its relation to the great movements in contemporary civilization as a whole. When we approach current history from this fundamental point of view, we perceive that the United States, along with the rest of the Western world, and much of the Orient as well, is passing through what we call the fourth great World Revolution in the historic experience of mankind.[1]

Our conception of a world-revolution is not limited to the violent changes which we usually associate with the word *revolution,* although, thus far in human experience, war and civil violence have accompanied the disintegration of old social orders and the inauguration of new ones.

By a world-revolution we mean a fundamental change in social institutions and patterns of life, and in the social and economic basis of the control over human society. A new class of leaders is thrown up. Either new institutions arise or sweeping changes are made in those which hold over from an earlier pattern of culture. A new type of civilization comes into being. The basic patterns of society are reconstructed.

At the Dawn of History in the ancient Near East, military chieftains from the earlier tribal society built up little feudal kingdoms and city-states. Adroit and powerful rulers of such political units conquered others and, in time, created kingdoms and empires. Vast wealth was amassed by rich landlords and a wealthy commercial class. A powerful priesthood, so it was thought, kept the favor of the gods and brought supernatural aid to the conquerors. The same process was repeated when the Roman Republic and the Roman Empire were created in later millenniums.

The second great world-revolution took place when Roman imperial society disintegrated after 300 A.D. and the Germanic tribal chieftains and kings seized control of Western Europe. They built a new social order founded primarily upon powerful landlords, thus creating what we know as medieval feudalism. In time, strong national monarchies arose, but nothing was brought forth which reproduced the great empires of classical antiquity. The manors and guilds dominated economic life, and

Catholic ethics controlled business and financial practices. The Catholic Church and Scholastic philosophy reigned supreme in the intellectual realm.

Following 1500, a third world-revolution came along, this time propelled chiefly by the rising power of the merchant class —the new bourgeoisie. At first, they supported the kings against their old traditional enemies, the feudal lords, thus promoting the growth of royal absolutism. However, the kings became an even greater menace to the mercantile classes than the feudal lords had once been; so the bourgeoisie took up arms against the kings and either displaced them or subordinated them to a system of representative government dominated by the middle-class merchants and businessmen.

The wars of Cromwell against Charles I, the ousting of James II, the American Revolutionary War, and the wars of the French Revolution and Napoleon were only incidental military episodes in the great social revolution, in the course of which the merchant class replaced the feudal landlords as the dominant class in western society. Napoleon, in any profound historical sense, was only an agent of social change hastening the process, as Stalin and Hitler sped up the fourth great world revolution in the course of which managerial bureaucrats or proletarian leaders may oust the moguls of capitalism in the dominion of society.

This third world-revolution which produced modern times probably bears the closest resemblance to our age. In the three centuries following 1500, the typical medieval institutions (such as a decentralized feudal government, an agricultural economy operated according to the manorial technique, the guild control of urban industry, local markets and national fairs to facilitate exchange of goods, the theory of the just price and other moral limitations on greed and sharp business practices, the great unified international Roman Catholic ecclesiastical state, and the Scholastic system of education) were undermined or completely supplanted.

In their place arose the basic institutions of the early modern age—the centralized national state, at first absolutistic and then representative, farming by free tenants under great landlords, an increasingly commercial and industrial economy, the domestic or putting-out system of industrial control, national and world trade, capitalistic ideals and methods, the quest of private profits by any means not flagrantly illegal, the great schism in the Catholic world-state produced by Protestantism, and the ascendancy of Humanistic ideals in education.

Had a scholar suggested in 1500 that the civilization of his age was about to undergo a sweeping transformation, he would have been ignored or ridiculed. But just this thing happened. By 1800, medieval civilization was no more, except in the more backward parts of Europe.

So, in the second third of the twentieth century, it is hard to believe that we may be in about the same situation in which the Western world found itself around 1500. Yet, plenty of evidence supports the opinion that more far-reaching changes have already been instituted since 1900 than any previous century has ever witnessed—perhaps the most fundamental transition in man's experience. We are already far advanced in the fourth great world revolution which will either bring man into an unprecedented era of peace, plenty and security or will produce world chaos and return us to barbarism. The outcome will depend entirely upon whether or not we are able to bring our institutions up to date and thereby enable us to utilize our great scientific and mechanical resources for the benefit of mankind rather than for the impoverishment and destruction of humanity.

The chief cause of these world revolutions has always been a discrepancy or maladjustment between material and non-material culture. At the Dawn of History, improvements in tools and weapons upset the simple life of tribal communities and started mankind on the march to conquest and the creation of larger settled societies. In ancient pagan civilization, social and cultural developments outran scientific and technological achievements. Especially was this true of the problems of imperial administration in ancient Rome, which lacked our modern methods of communication and transportation.

As the Middle Ages wore on, the long bow and gunpowder helped to end feudalism. Better farming implements increased the crop output and made it possible to farm for profit. The horse-collar and iron-rimmed cartwheels improved land transport. The mechanical fulling-machine facilitated woolen manufactures. The mastery of nautical instruments and the building of ships which permitted ocean travel uprooted medieval provincialism, stimulated the expansion of Europe, and brought the modern world into being. Then came the rise of modern science and engineering and the three Industrial Revolutions which have given us modern industry, transportation and communication thus completely changing the whole nature of our material culture and ways of living.

Never before has there been such a gulf between technology and social institutions as in our own day. We have a thoroughly up-to-date science and material culture, diverse, and potentially efficient beyond that of any earlier age. On the other hand, the institutions and the social thinking through which we seek to control and exploit this material culture are an antiquated mosaic, compounded of accretions from the Stone Age to the close of the eighteenth century.

It is, therefore, quite obvious that the key to the understanding of the reasons for the decay of modern institutions, the decline of our civilization, and the precipitation of the fourth world revolution lies in the phenomenal growth of contemporary science and technology and the failure of our institutional life and social thinking to keep pace with these startlingly rapid and complex changes in our material life. The striking developments associated with aviation—jet planes that can encircle the globe in a few hours—the atom bomb, and the like, are only the more recent and dramatic aspects of the manner in which our mechanical world has forged ahead of our social institutions. These recent developments have shocked some persons into consciousness that something is wrong in the picture of contemporary life, but few understand the real nature or extent of the problems which are involved.

This ever-widening gulf between our science and technology on the one hand, and our institutional development and social thinking, on the other, is what we call "Cultural Lag," following the phraseology which Professor William F. Ogburn introduced a generation ago in his book, *Social Change*. We may illustrate its character and extent by comparing some of our leading institutions with our up-to-the-minute achievements in the field of science and technology.

II. CULTURAL LAG: UP-TO-DATE MACHINES AND ANTIQUE INSTITUTIONS

The preceding pages have made it evident that the outstanding reason why the Western world, and as much of the Eastern world as has been affected by Western civilization, has come into a critical revolutionary situation is that our scientific knowledge and material culture have tended greatly to outdistance the institutional patterns of life through which we seek to operate and control an era of scientific miracles and mechanical marvels. In the field of science we have established the doctrine of evolution, mastered the mysteries of electro-mechanics, laid bare the chemical facts of life and industry, created quantum physics and relativity, and, finally, have unleashed the vast and unpredictable forces of intra-atomic energy.[2]

The progress of mechanical invention has been as striking and immense as the advances in science. The first Industrial Revolution, which started in England about 1750, created our modern methods of textile manufacturing, the new iron and steel industry, the steam engine, and the beginning of steam transport on land and sea. The first Industrial Revolution had hardly been established in many countries before a second came on its heels. This introduced the application of chemistry in the steel, rubber, oil, and other industries, along with creating synthetic products of many kinds, brought about new methods of transportation and communication, and set up large-scale industrial establishments. Today we are in the midst of the third Industrial Revolution—the age of electrification, automatic machinery, electric control over manufacturing processes, air transport, radios, and so on. With the coming of intra-atomic energy and supersonic stratosphere aviation we face an even more staggering fourth Industrial Revolution.

We have giant turbines, four of which can generate more energy than the whole working population of the United States. We possess automatic machinery of the most amazing efficiency. One plant can, for example, turn out 650,000 light bulbs each day or 10,000 times as many per man as was possible by the older methods. This automatic machinery can be controlled by thermostats and the photo-electric cell, or "electric eye," which are absolutely dependable and unfailing and all but eliminate the human factor in those forms of mechanical production where they can be utilized. We have giant auto buses; clean, quiet, speedy Diesel-motored trains; safe, swift airplanes. We have enormous skyscrapers. Our bathrooms would fill a Roman emperor with envy. Our system of communication is incredibly extensive and efficient. Our radios would appear a miracle to persons who died so recently as the period of the first World War. Radar and its uses is even more striking and momentous in its nature and possibilities. Our modern printing presses would stagger Gutenberg. We could thus go on indefinitely through all the provinces of our great "Empire of Machines."

We have thus built up an impressive and up-to-date material culture, diverse, complex, and potentially efficient beyond that of any other age. Yet, little of our institutional equipment through which we seek to operate in an atomic age dates from a period more recent than the days of George Washington and Thomas Jefferson. We can demonstrate this by briefly reviewing the main social institutions of our era and indicating the dates at which they made their entry into our cultural complex.

To begin with our economic life, our basic economic institution is capitalism and the profit system. This came into existence as a result of the Protestant Revolution, the expansion of Europe and the Commercial Revolution of the sixteenth and seventeenth centuries. It was so well developed by the eighteenth century that what is often regarded as its classic exposition and defense was set forth in 1776 by Adam Smith in his famous *Wealth of Nations.* To be sure, capitalism has undergone some mutations since 1800, but most of the basic philosophy and practices of capitalism were extant and relatively mature by that time.

Our leading political institutions are equally venerable. The national state, the fundamental political framework of our day, had come into existence by the seventeenth century and was accorded formal political and legal status in the Treaty of Westphalia in 1648. Representative government had triumphed in England by 1689. The English Levellers had worked out a more comprehensive and radical theory of democracy than the New Deal away back in the time of Cromwell. Democratic practices were introduced in our colonial town meeting of the seventeenth and eighteenth centuries, and democracy became legally triumphant in this country over a hundred years ago. The theories and practices of the common law, natural law and constitutional law, which still control our legal life and thought, were all well developed by the close of the seventeenth century in England.

Our religious institutions are even more archaic than those which control our political and economic life. Christianity had its immediate origins nearly 2,000 years ago, and it drew a great deal not only from Jewish and other religions which were then thousands of years old, but also from the primitive religious rites and beliefs that lay back of the Dawn of History. Protestantism diverged only slightly in doctrine from Catholicism and it came into being back in the sixteenth century. Our ethical beliefs and practices have been intimately associated with our religious life and dogmas and are fully as antique in their background and conceptions.

Education is also a strange mosaic of antiquities. Much of our educational ideology and curriculum comes down from primitive society and ancient times. Most of our educational nomenclature and ritual, as well as some of the subject-matter of the curriculum, come from the Middle Ages. Our so-called liberal education is derived chiefly from the proposals of the Italian educational reformers of the fifteenth and sixteenth centuries. We vainly attempt to apply this as the means of training our children to live under democracy in the nineteenth and twentieth centuries. Even Progressive Education is mainly a rationalization and elaboration of the educational doctrines of an eighteenth-century writer, Jean Jacques Rousseau.

It is quite obvious that no civilization can endure and prosper with such an alarming disparity between the two great aspects of its structure and life processes. It is this wide abyss between our material culture and our social institutions which has brought on the fourth world revolution and forced upon us the necessity of either making constructive readjustments or facing social chaos and cultural disintegration.

III. HOW CULTURAL LAG CREATED THE PUBLIC PROBLEMS AND SOCIAL CRISES OF OUR DAY

It was inevitable that the wide gap between our material culture and our institutional life which we have described above would create critical public problems in the operation of our society. By the second decade of the twentieth century our leading modern institutions began to show signs of impairment and disintegration as menacing as those in the Western Roman Empire in the time of Diocletian. There was no longer any doubt that fundamental readjustments must be made. The only question was whether they would be brought about by rational and peaceful methods or through violence and revolution.[3]

In the economic field, capitalism has failed to give humanity anything like the full benefits of potential mechanical production. Capitalism has been degraded by excessive devotion to the profit motive, and has indulged in great wastes while failing to provide adequate mass purchasing-power. It has developed into a system which seeks to market a restricted volume of the poorest quality of permanently salable goods or services for the highest obtainable returns. Traditional labor unionists learned this pattern of behavior from the capitalists and have countered by demanding the highest wages they can secure for the shortest possible working day, in which, in some cases, as much loafing and restriction of output as can be "gotten away with" is the order of the day. The public is ground between these two millstones of class greed, which jointly restrict the possibility of attaining and enjoying the economy of abundance which our machines have made possible.

The type of capitalism which has become dominant is finance

capitalism, controlled by great investment bankers who are more immediately interested in financial speculation and manipulation than in operating an efficient industrial structure and securing legitimate profits therefrom. Ownership is divorced from management, with a resulting development of managerial irresponsibility and excessive salaries for a padded officialdom. More interest is shown by the leaders of finance capitalism in looting corporations from the inside through holding companies and other predatory devices than in providing them with expert management. Monopolies and "bottle-necks" restrict output, keep prices high, and place prosperity in jeopardy. The ideals and methods of the ancient scarcity economy have thus been perpetuated, while our new technology is geared to provide abundance.

In the overseas field, capitalism has encouraged reckless investment in foreign securities and enterprise, passing the risk on to gullible and ignorant investors who, in the end, "hold the bag" and are consigned to poverty and ruin. More than half of our foreign investments have gone into default of principal, interest, or both. Today, in our era of "Deficit Mercantilism," we do not even expect to get repayment for our foreign loans.

The speculative motives of finance capitalism have also come to control the older industrial capitalism, much of which is dominated by great corporations ruled by investment bankers. Waste and inefficiency have been rampant. Even in the years before the great depression of 1929, we wasted at least half of our potential productive capacity. We could have turned out twice as many goods as we did without any increase in plant. Even this grossly inadequate product could not be effectively marketed because capitalism was unwilling to provide sufficiently high wages and steady employment to create adequate purchasing power. The cost of food and goods to the underpaid masses has been inflated by the great increase in overhead charges developed under finance capitalism and modern advertising. This resulted in a situation where it costs more than twice as much to get food and goods to the consumer as it does to produce them.

There has been a fatal maladistribution of wealth and income. In 1929, the one-tenth of one percent of the families at the top of the income bracket in the United States received as much of the total national income as the poorest forty-two percent of the families in the nation. Conditions were not markedly different in other great capitalistic states. Capitalism has refused to assume the basic responsibility of "feeding its sheep." Unemployment became a desperate menace, except under an armament or war economy. Capitalistic irresponsibility and ever more efficient labor-saving mechanical inventions combined to throw millions out of work and to render them almost impotent as purchasers of the commodities produced by the empire of machines.

This lack of mass purchasing power, which was produced mainly by the concentration of wealth and income, has also paralyzed the prosperity of farmers. They obtained ever better machinery and were equipped to produce more crops, but those in our cities who needed more food did not have the money to buy it in adequate quantities. Even before the depression following 1929, about seventy-five percent of American families did not have income enough to buy the food needed to maintain what the government described as a decent standard of health. The Roman Empire had to strain every effort to raise enough food to supply its peoples, but in our day we have faced the spectacle of the starvation or hunger of countless millions in the face of great agricultural surpluses. These surpluses existed even with wasteful and inefficient methods of production. Had we made use of the most efficient known agricultural technology we could have produced far more than we did, with one-fifth of the agricultural labor actually employed and on one-fifth of the land under cultivation.

Our fundamental political institutions have proved as inadequate to the responsibilities of the machine age as finance capitalism and the profit system have in the economic realm. The national state, equipped with the communication facilities of the steam and electric age, has spread over great areas the same bellicosity and hostility that had once characterized old tribal groups. Equipped with the modern mechanism of warfare, these nations have threatened the peace and safety of all mankind. Modern nationalism, linked up with mechanized armies constitutes an unprecedented menace to civilization. Once we believed that we might find relief and safety from nationalism in internationalism, but in the years since 1937 the internationalists have become far more bellicose than the nationalists. Most of the wars and the international chaos since 1937 have been the work of the internationalists. They now seem to be working in every conceivable way to bring on a third World War.

The national state also brought about almost insuperable problems in the task of providing wise legislation and competent administration. As life became more complex after the Industrial Revolutions, it became ever more difficult to administer such great political entities as national states by means of representative government, democracy and political parties. Due to the inefficiency of these institutions, critical conditions arose which invited the more drastic methods of dictatorship and totalitarianism.

Democratic government was placed in serious jeopardy because the increase in the number, variety and difficulty of the problems to be handled has not been paralleled by a comparable effort to secure greater expertness and honesty in public office. Democracy was originally conceived of and recommended for the government of small states in an agricultural and pastoral stage of civilization. By making proper modifications and improvements, it might have been rendered adequate to controlling the problems of an urban and industrial world civilization. But nowhere have such reforms been introduced with sufficient rapidity and thoroughness to keep pace with the increasing problems and responsibilities of governmental action.

The original exponents of democracy believed that the masses would take an active interest in government, once they had the right to vote, and would be alert to choose able rulers. These expectations have not been borne out in experience. In the United States only about half of the people legally qualified to vote go to the polls, even under the pressure of the excitement generated by a presidential campaign. The people have also shown great apathy about careful study of politics, and the powerful economic interests have been able to place their servants and stooges in the more responsible posts of government. Rarely have democracies been able to provide gifted and independent leadership with any continuity. Nor have they built up an educational system adequate to equip the mass of citizens with the knowledge needed to operate a democracy. While all children have been enabled to go to school at public expense, the subject-matter taught them stems essentially from that approved for children of the nobility in a decaying feudal society.

Closely related to the failure of traditional democracy to cope with the public problems of modern life is the inefficiency and corruption of party government. Party activities are conducted primarily upon the basis of emotions and venality, rather than as a rational means of efficient government. The appeal of party leaders is to emotion and self-interest. Party machines are corrupt, indulge in extensive graft, and betray the people in the interest of partisan entrenchment and in the service of powerful economic interests and predatory minorities. The best that political parties can produce are politicians, who are veritable experts in getting elected and then preparing to get themselves re-elected. But such expertness has little to do with statecraft, namely, expertness in governing after one is elected. Parties have become an end in themselves rather than a means of serving the public. They have become autocratic in their management and are thus antagonistic to democratic ideals and principles. In some countries they have, as *blocs,* become so numerous as to paralyze parliamentary government. When this happens, dictatorships may spring up and institute a one-party system which suppresses democracy and true representative government.

Representative government and democracy have also proved incompetent in handling international relations. Democracies have shown just as great a willingness to resort to war as dictatorships. They have been just as unwilling to disarm and entrust international relations to arbitration and peaceful adjustment. They learned no lessons from the first World War but plunged recklessly ahead into a second World War along with the dictatorships, and are today taking the lead in seeking to precipitate the third World War.

Nor have the democracies shown any greater integrity in diplomacy than was characteristic of the old monarchies. Secret diplomacy and diplomatic double-crossing have continued to be the order of the day. Diplomats deceive the people rather than serving them. What little good faith previously existed between nations has disappeared, and the twentieth century became, as Lamar Middleton has put it, the era of "the twilight of treaties." Not a single major treaty made between the first and second World Wars was honored by its signatories when it was to their interest to break it. Even the international treaty to renounce war—the so-called Kellogg Pact—was conceived in sham and dedicated to hypocrisy.

The second World War, which, in its final results, may possibly end the historic experiment with democracy, was, in one sense, a logical proof of the inefficiency and dishonesty of democracies in world affairs. Any dictatorial threat to peace and integrity might easily have been checked had the powerful democracies acted with efficiency and honesty at any time from 1933 to 1938. And primary responsibility for the needless physical destruction in the second World War and for the economic, social and moral chaos following VJ Day must be assigned to the leaders of the democracies—notably for the Casablanca Unconditional Surrender slogan and for the Morgenthau Plan and the Potsdam agreement that have wrecked Europe and laid it wide open to the inroads of Communism.

Liberty is in the same critical situation today as our other social institutions. It is interesting, and also somewhat disconcerting, to note that there have been few significant advances in our conceptions and categories of liberty since the Bill of Rights of 1689 and the days of John Locke, at the close of the seventeenth century. Roger Baldwin and the American Civil Liberties Union are still battling to protect the liberties which were won for us in the seventeenth century and outlined in the English Bill of Rights of 1689.

No branch of our institutional life is more incompetent and stereotyped than our law. Religion may be even more archaic in its concepts, but its failures are not so immediately disastrous to the operation of our institutions and the security of our lives. Highly competent lawyers have charged that our legal system creates more litigation than it settles and brings about far more injustice than justice. As Newman Levy, a distinguished New York attorney puts it: "We hear much talk about justice. In the abstract it is a beautiful and desirable concept. But justice, *per se,* plays a small part in the daily activities of the busy practitioner." Indeed, some realistic lawyers have contended that the defects of the law today are so serious that if they are not eliminated they may provoke civil war. Not only is law archaic in itself, but it is very effective in holding back the evolution of many other institutions, thus contributing powerfully to that general cultural lag which has already placed civilization in jeopardy. The professional lawyers have been called the strategists of social stagnation and cultural lag.

Education, which was the great hope of reformers of the eighteenth-century Enlightenment, has failed to live up to their expectations. We have already pointed out that our educators persist in giving to our "little democrats" the type of information which was originally designed for the children of a decadent feudal age. Organized education makes little effort to criticize the social order and to suggest drastic improvements therein. It tends to sanctify things as they are and thus actually constitutes a powerful obstacle to planned changes within the democratic structure of society. It had been the idea of Lester F. Ward and others that organized education would impel and guide desirable social change and social reform. But, actually, it has tended, preponderantly, to retard planned social advances. By obstructing orderly progress, education plays its part in inviting the violence and revolution which almost inevitably arise whenever change and readjustment are too long delayed.

Even much-touted educational reforms, such as the Adler-Hutchins-St. John's program that revolves about the study of a "Hundred Great Books"—mostly antique treatises—are even more of a retreat from reality than the conventional curriculum. Such programs veritably glory and wallow in cultural lag.

Orthodox religion and conventional morals are little different in fundamentals from what they were in the Middle Ages and early modern times. They remain primarily concerned with adjusting us to the hypothetical supernatural world and in assuring a blessed immortality in the world to come. They give relatively little attention to the matter of promoting happiness, well-being, justice and peace here on earth. Those in a state of economic desperation therefore look less and less to churchmen and more and more to secular messiahs for relief and enrichment.

IV. HOW OUR PRESENT STATE OF ALARMING CULTURAL LAG CAME ABOUT

A little reflection on the history of modern times makes it easy to understand how this dangerous disparity between our material culture and our social institutions has come about. It is not, as some suppose, because our institutional development in modern times has been slower than in earlier ages. As a matter of fact, institutional progress has been more rapid since 1500 than in any other comparable period of human history.[4]

The most important factor that has brought about the great gulf between machines and institutions is the fact that especially since about 1750, science and machinery have gone ahead with a rapidity never dreamed of before. There has been greater scientific and mechanical progress since 1450 than in the whole million or more years of human experience before modern times. Institutional development, even though relatively rapid in the last five centuries, has simply not been able to keep pace with scientific and mechanical progress. Another important element in the situation is that, as we shall see, the business classes have, particularly since about 1800, thrown the whole weight of their influence behind stimulating science and machinery, while they have, at the same time, sought to stabilize institutions and frustrate social change.

In early modern times, there was actually a greater social impulse to institutional changes and to new types of social thought than there was to the progress of science and invention. Between 1450 and 1750, as the Middle Ages came to an end and modern times came into being, these changes were mainly the product of the policies of the middle class. The middle class repudiated most types of medieval institutions and social thought. It helped along the growth of the national state and transformed it from an absolutistic to a representative basis. It developed the ideas of natural law, which placed jurisprudence behind the protection of property. In conjunction with the Protestant leaders the middle class created and fostered the capitalistic system and the eulogy of pecuniary profits. It took an active part in colonialism and the creation of modern imperialism; developed an appropriate type of political and economic theory to justify the new bourgeois system; and brought into being the liberal political philosophy which justified revolution against the privileged aristocracy, and defended outstanding civil liberties, such as freedom of speech, press, assemblage, religion, and the like. In economics, it extolled the freedom of trade and the immunity of business and trade from extensive governmental regulation. These institutional changes were far more rapid and extensive than the mechanical advances between 1450 and 1750.

Most of these innovations in economics and politics had been achieved by the close of the eighteenth century. The system thus created by the middle class tended thereafter to crystallize and to resist change. In this way, the social class which, between 1450 and 1750, had strongly encouraged the transformation of institutions and social thought, became an insuperable obstacle to further changes in the nineteenth and twentieth centuries. After it had built the new, or bourgeois, social order, the middle class believed that its interests were linked up with preserving the status quo in institutional life and social thought.

Hence, the business and financial classes threw all of their tremendous power into the maintenance of things as they were in our institutional life. This they did at the very time when they were becoming ever more enthusiastic in the way of promoting progress in science and technology. Therefore, from about 1800 to the present time, the dominating economic groups in modern society have tended to resist social and institutional change, while at the same time they have encouraged advances in science and technology. This is the main reason for the strange and alarming state of affairs which we face today; namely, the juxtaposition of a thoroughly up-to-date science and technology and a heritage of social institutions and social thought which date, for the most part, from around 1800 or earlier. Conditions in our modern world have, for more than a century, worked strongly, on the one hand, to encourage scientific and mechanical advance, and, on the other hand, to produce institutional stability.

Another reason why material culture advances far more rapidly than social institutions in our day is that material culture has become far more thoroughly secularized than our institutional equipment. Therefore, there is nothing like the same emotional and quasi-religious opposition to changes in science and machinery as there is to any proposal to alter our social institutions.

In primitive times, material culture was also regarded as sacred and revealed by the gods. While it was, perhaps, not so completely holy and sanctified as social institutions, yet material culture—tools, weapons, and the like—was venerated, and the innovator placed himself in jeopardy if he proposed the use of a new tool or weapon. Primitive peoples often adhered to obviously inferior material equipment for fear that they might offend the gods, and material progress was slowed down by this "technological piety." There were exceptions but only enough to prove the rule.

Gradually, however, the superstitious element in the field of material culture was reduced in later primitive society, and it was the invention of superior tools and weapons that carried mankind from tribal society to the origins of "civilization" at the Dawn of History. By modern times, the notion of the sanctity of any particular pattern of material culture had been pretty well broken down, and science and machinery had become essentially secularized. There were some attenuated hangovers for generations, well represented by the fantastic opposition to new methods of transportation, such as railroads. Nevertheless, by and large, the secularization of science and technology was well advanced by early modern times and the completion of this process is one of the outstanding accomplishments of modern civilization. We are no longer fearful of the gods or evil spirits if we discard an ancient tool, vehicle or machine and choose a newer and more efficient one.

In contrast with this, we find that social institutions still retain much the same halo of sanctity with which they were endowed in primitive society. While we may not fear so directly the vengeance of the gods, if we alter a social institution, as was the case in primitive days, we act as though we did. We appear to assume that, if we change the social pattern of life, some horrible disaster will result, even if the gods do not obliterate the nation. This was well illustrated, as late as 1937, by the popular horror at the proposal to reform the Supreme Court. While part of this apparent terror was drummed up by cynical politicians and economic reactionaries to discredit the Roosevelt administration, there were millions who sincerely believed that the Court was invested with some sort of divinity and that to alter its composition and challenge its tyranny would bring social chaos to the country. No sort of propaganda, however clever and lavishly subsidized could have raised a similar outcry about any change in material culture. Henry Ford's change of his automobile from Model T to Model A was greeted with nation-wide eagerness and enthusiasm.

Hence, while we find little or no emotional or superstitious opposition to scientific discoveries and mechanical inventions today, we still have to work against the popular hypothesis that social institutions are sacred and venerable and that to alter them, or even propose to alter them significantly, is wicked and nefarious and a dangerous challenge to social well-being.

Still another reason why a great gulf has developed between our material culture and our institutional heritage is to be found in our simian ancestry, a consideration which is one of the leading contributions of Darwinism to social enlightenment. Monkeys are curious about material things and are much given to "fussing" around with their hands—to "monkeying." This is especially true of the higher apes that stand closest to mankind. Along with man, they are "handy." Now, handiness is the mother of invention, and man received from his general siamian heritage his talent for inventiveness in the material realm. Apes invent relatively little and do not pass on any of their inventions. But the handiness that man inherits from his simian ancestry, in conjunction with his greater brain power, have enabled him to invent many things and to pass these inventions on to later generations. Man's superior power to imitate has helped him along in this achievement. Ultimately, human handiness produced the wonders of modern technology.

In marked contrast to simian handiness is the disinclination of simians to indulge in abstractions. There have been literally billions of men who were "handy" in the realm of material things since the appearance of mankind on the planet, but there have not been more than a few hundred outstanding philosophers, namely, those who are adept in abstractions. Men are far more interested in gadgets than in abstract thought. Social philosophy and social planning lie in the field of abstractions and, hence, are not enthusiastically cultivated by a race of simian ancestry.

This means that, as simians, men are interested in, and adept at material things and the alterations thereof, while they are notoriously indifferent to, and incompetent at, social thought and social planning. In short, our biological heritage naturally impels us to occupy ourselves with material things and discourages or frustrates intelligent interest in analyzing, evaluating and altering, for the better, our institutional equipment.

V. WHY WE FAIL TO CLOSE THE GULF BETWEEN MACHINES AND INSTITUTIONS

If the gulf between machines and institutions is the chief cause of current difficulties and disasters, from poverty to war, it may seem surprising that so little is being done to remedy this situation. But a little resort to social psychology and cultural history is quite sufficient to explain our lamentable defects and failures in this respect.[5]

One of the most conspicuous things about the mental life of our day is the contrast in our attitude toward modernity and efficiency in science and machinery, on the one hand, and in institutions and social thought, on the other. It is frequently asserted that we are all living today in a scientific age. The fact is, of course, that we are not doing anything of the sort, so far as the attitudes of the average citizen are concerned. Modern civilization is a venerable institutional parasite, unintelligently exploiting the products of contemporary science and technology.

The mass of mankind in Western civilization have been, it is true, vastly affected in an indirect way by the progress of nineteenth and twentieth century science. New mechanical devices and conveniences have vitally altered people's lives. Men are healed of diseases more surely and more often and operated upon by surgeons more successfully and more painlessly. In popular magazines and newspapers they read superficially about the wonders that modern science has uncovered. They look through bigger and better telescopes, and through powerful microscopes, to instruct or amuse themselves with respect to the expanse of the heavens or the minute wonders of the animal and vegetable worlds.

The basic attitudes of the average man in the Western world have, however, been very slightly altered by the direct impact of science. To be sure, the perspective of a man who has traveled across a continent in a streamlined railroad train or transcontinental airliner must be somewhat different from that of one whose travels were confined to an ox-cart within a rural township. But a transcontinental railroad trip may not prevent a person from viewing the fundamental problems of life and society much as his grandfather did two generations before while jogging along in his buggy.

Such is the situation with Western civilization as a whole. In their thinking about God, the world, man, politics, law, wealth and economics, education and the problems of right and wrong, most men are as much dominated by custom, tradition, folklore and habit in the 1940's as they were in the 1640's. The power of the supernatural over human thought has been little affected by scientific progress. Tradition and emotion, rather than fact and logic, prevail. Belief and conviction remain supreme.

Our opinions and institutions are overwhelmingly the product of contributions from the pre-scientific era. In our age, civilization has been profoundly affected in certain respects by scientific discoveries and their application to our material culture. Mankind, still primarily pre-scientific in its thinking and life-interests, has thus been able to appropriate the results of the investigations and achievements of a few scientifically-minded pioneers. Probably fewer than 500 individuals have been mainly responsible for the changes in material civilization that separate us from the days of Columbus and Luther.

Very often those who most greedily accept and enjoy the products of modern science and technology engage in attacks upon the scientific approach to life. Not infrequently, persons who are most exacting in their demands for the most recent provisions in plumbing, the best medical attention, the most efficient and up-to-date automobiles, at the same time defend classical or medieval civilization as the ideal period of human development. Many an industrialist, financier or labor leader, traveling in a modern clipper plane, is at the same time disporting an intellect which could be matched in most respects by the mental attitudes of a cave-dweller in the late Paleolithic period, or at least by those of Tecumseh or Sitting Bull.

We desire, and, if we have money enough to buy them, we get for ourselves the latest in automobiles, radios, plumbing and electrical gadgets. We are humiliated by any evidence that we are behind the times in such matters. The average American would be greatly embarrassed to drive a reconditioned 1925 touring car through the thoroughfares of any of our main cities. This would be the case, even if the car were in new condition. The mere fact that its model was two decades or so out of date would provide sharp humiliation for the owner.

But the very person who would be embarrassed by a motor car two decades behind the times is likely to demonstrate great enthusiasm, if not sheer reverence, for a constitution a century and a half old, or for an economic system which was already being extolled by Adam Smith in the year 1776. The man who expresses great contempt for the transportation ideals of the horse-and-buggy era usually defends with gusto and conviction political and economic ideas which long antedate the stagecoach.

This situation makes it very difficult to do anything to bridge the gulf between machines and institutions. So long as we are proud of our institutions and ideas in direct ratio to the antiquity of their origin, we have less than any incentive to bring them up-to-date. Until we are as much embarrassed by an archaic idea or social practice as we are by an obsolete gadget there is little prospect of making any headway in the modernization of our institutional equipment. Nor is there much prospect that we will do so until we are just as insistent in demanding experts in legislative halls and administrative offices as we are today in assuring their presence in power plants, garages and hospitals.

Far from taking steps to bridge the gulf by bringing our institutions up-to-date, the intellectual attitudes and social values of our era actually tend to widen the gulf. We provide all sorts of prizes for scientists and engineers who make important discoveries—even though we stand in no great present need of further scientific discoveries, save perhaps in the field of medicine. Nor do we actually require any additional mechanical inventions. What we need, more than anything else today, are the contributions of the social inventors—those men who can bring our institutions and social thinking up to date by devising new and better forms of government, economic life, legal practices, moral codes, and educational systems.

But we have few or no prizes or rewards for the social inventor. At best, he is likely to be ridiculed as a well-meaning crank or "nitwit." In certain countries he may be imprisoned or shot. The net result of all this is an extension of the already menacing abyss between our science and machinery and our institutional life and social thought.

It is not surprising, then, to find a sharp contrast between the type of guidance which we demand in the field of science and technology and that with which we rest satisfied in regard to our institutional procedure. We insist upon the very finest medical scientists and surgeons we can afford. We would be inexpressibly shocked at the suggestion that we should call in, for an operation, the family butcher, who might possess remarkable facility as an adroit meatcutter. When there is an operation to be performed upon the human body, we wish the most competent "brain trust" we can obtain. But, for operations upon the body politic, with problems far more complex and technical than any conceivable surgical operation upon the human body, we continue to allow ignorant and venal political butchers to hack and mangle the body politic at their will. Men like Harding, Coolidge or Truman, who were called upon to guide the destinies of the greatest nation on earth in the two most critical and complex periods of its history, rate in scientific statecraft about as a chiropractor or a Christian Science healer would rank in the field of medicine and surgery. Hence, we need not be surprised at the vast amount of bungling which goes on in contemporary public life. Until we are as willing and eager to call in experts to guide us in our institutional life as we are to seek the service of medical experts or to demand experts to repair our gadgets, there is little hope that we shall be able to deal effectively with the complex problems of contemporary life.

The discrepancy which exists between our machines, on the one hand, and our institutions and social thinking, on the other, is of the greatest importance in any attempt to understand the social problems of our age. The latter are, without exception, only incidental manifestations of the gulf between machines and institutions, no matter what type of social problem with which we deal. We may illustrate this point by reference to several leading public problems, starting first with the economic problem of scarcity and insecurity in the face of technological ability to produce an abundance of food and goods.

While millions suffered, were on relief, or were ill-fed and ill-clothed in the United States in 1933, the government paid farmers to plow under wheat and cotton, leaving less to eat and wear. Millions have been on relief or in the bread-lines at a moment when the factories and farms were well equipped to turn out an abundance of goods and food. Despite all the waste, our productive potentialities are equipped to give us all we need in every field of human requirements. But the distributive ideals and processes of society possess nothing like the same facility in putting goods at the disposal of consumers.

This paradox is, however, easily explained. The productive side of our economic life, based primarily upon our science and machinery, is *relatively* up to date and efficient. The ideas and practices which control distribution and consumption are, on the contrary, a manifestation and reflection of our laggard institutional life and social thinking, which are highly retarded, out-of-date, and ineffective. If we possessed the same efficiency in getting goods to eager consumers that we possess in turning them out in our factories, there would be no economic crisis in modern industry. Our clumsy and outworn economic system exacts a cost of over two dollars ($2.34 in 1938) to get to the consumers each dollar's worth of goods purchased at the farm or factory gate. If we could get food to the hungry masses as readily and cheaply as the farmers can provide it, there would be no crisis in agriculture, no millions denied the primary necessities of existence.

Another instance is the case of medical science and medical care. Medical science has made completely revolutionary progress in the last half century. There is little resemblance between the diagnosis and therapy of 1900 and that of 1947. Yet the application of medical science to humanity—medical care—operates within much the same patterns of policy and ideas and the same framework of practice that it did in 1847. The highly trained physician or surgeon of today plies his craft in harmony with the ideas of medical care which were carried out by "the horse-and-buggy doctor." The result is that only a small fraction of the population receives the medical care which could be made available in the light of contemporary medical knowledge and the medical resources of the country—and at no greater cost than what is expended for the grossly inadequate medical care of our day.

For another striking contrast, let us take the example of war in contemporary times. When it comes to devising and manufacturing bigger and better machinery for the destruction of humanity, we are able to produce ever better battleships, submarines, tanks, dive-bombers, bomb-sights, automatic rifles, machine-guns, tommy-guns, field and long-range artillery, blockbusters and atom bombs. There seems to be no limit to the intelligence which we apply to the technical problem of war. We pool every intellectual resource of university laboratories, scientific foundations, and industrial research to discover how we may wage war more effectively.

On the other hand, we approach the whole social and cultural problem of war with attitudes dating back to the period of bows and arrows and the battle-axe, if not the fist-hatchet. We do not apply even sixth-grade intelligence to studying the problem of how we might rid the world of the menace of war. Whatever social services war may have rendered in early days, it has now become a fatal anachronism and the chief threat to the preservation of contemporary civilization. It does not require even grammar-school intelligence to see that the institution of war is a stupid monstrosity. Yet the very best brains of the world are still employed to facilitate and extend its deadly ravages. As matters now stand, our failure to bridge the gulf between devastating war machinery and our institutional approach to the war problem may ultimately wipe out human civilization with atom bombs and atom rockets.

This discussion of war as an example of cultural lag brings us to the heart of the whole matter. For a long time the issue of cultural lag has been of great practical importance. The failure to modernize our institutions has been responsible for nearly all of the public problems and social evils of our age. Cultural lag has produced our economic problems of waste, under-consumption, low standards of living, poverty, unemployment and the like. It accounts for our inadequate housing, much unnecessary disease, sickness and death. It is what has produced most of the wars in contemporary times and prevented really adequate and constructive plans for peace.

Nevertheless, despite all these handicaps and evils produced by cultural lag, humanity could survive in the past. But the arrival of intra-atomic energy and the atom bomb have introduced an altogether new and more alarming phase into the situation. This time, and from now onward, the lessening and elimination of cultural lag involve the very survival of the human race. Unless we are able to bring up to date the institutions which are most directly involved in the causes and prevention of war it will not be long before humanity will be partly extinguished and the remainder consigned to barbarism, as Lewis Mumford pointed out in striking but accurate fashion in the March 1947 issue of *Air Affairs*. As Mumford makes clear, even if there is no third war with atomic weapons, the fear of such a war may force a type of life and regimentation which will be little better than barbarism. And were the atom bomb to be discarded, there would remain just as terrible possibilities of destruction in the new poison gases and bacterial warfare. Nothing short of an institutional readjustment sufficient to hold all wars in check—and that without barbarizing fears and preparations—will suffice to preserve anything deserving the name of civilization. Otherwise, cultural lag will exact its final penalty in the destruction of human civilization just as physiological maladjustments once doomed the dinosaurs.

VI. CONCLUSION

The preceding pages have made it clear that the great problem of our era is the disparity between modern science and technology, on the one hand, and our social institutions on the other.

And no program for peace, security and prosperity will suffice unless it envisages and secures a sufficient bridging of the gulf between machines and institutions to end economic waste and warfare. Anything short of this can be no more than mere temporizing—dealing with symptoms of our basic disorders rather than with the fundamental causes. And the arrival of the atom bomb emphasizes the fact that we cannot expect slowly to muddle through with any such program. It must be put through speedily enough so that it can be successful before a third World War breaks out or before the fear of such a war has destroyed all possibility of creative activity and social invention. The problem is clear, but the time is short.

It will avail nothing to retreat from the issue into the fog of mysticism which is proving so popular with those who lack the courage to face the issues and consequences produced by our scientific laboratories and empire of machines. Dodging the issue through metaphysical and mystical befogging of our thought has been a main reason for the alarming growth of cultural lag, until it now threatens racial extinction. Less than nothing will be gained by seeking refuge in dogmatic cults or in the mystical writings of a Toynbee or Sorokin. We must face the problems with the resolute courage of men like the late H. G. Wells who saw that scientific and mechanical marvels can bring untold benefits to mankind if we will but learn how to use them for the advantage of the race and to face social problems with the clarity and directness of science.[6]

---

1. For the factual basis of the four world revolutions, see H. E. Barnes, *History of Western Civilizations*, 2 vols., Harcourt, Brace, 1935; and for the fourth world revolution, Vol. II, Part III.
2. Barnes, *Social Institutions*, Prentice-Hall, 1942, Part I; and *An Economic History of the Western World* (New York: Harcourt, Brace, 1937), Parts IV-V.
3. Barnes, *Social Institutions, passim;* and *A Survey of Western Civilization,* Crowell, 1947, Part VIII.

4. Barnes, *Can Man Be Civilized?* Brentano, 1932.
5. James Harvey Robinson, *The Mind in the Making,* Harper, 1921; *The Humanizing of Knowledge,* Doran, 1923; *The Human Comedy,* Harper, 1937.
6. G. A. Lundberg, *Can Science Save Us?* (New York: Longmans, 1947); J. E. Thornton, ed., *Science and Social Change* (Washington: Brookings Institution, 1939); and R. N. Anshen, ed., *Science and Man* (New York: Harcourt, Brace, 1942).

CHAPTER XI

THE THEORY OF PROGRESS IN HISTORICAL AND SOCIOLOGICAL PERSPECTIVE

I. THE NATURE OF PROGRESS

Our discussion of cultural lag brings us directly to a consideration of the theory and reality of progress.[1] By progress, in its social implications, we mean a definite improvement in the well-being of human society. It implies a discernible advance in the enlightenment, prosperity, and security of mankind. Progress takes on many forms: intellectual, aesthetic, and material. It involves an increase of knowledge and a greater command of the mind over the realities and problems of life. Aesthetic progress envisages more attention and competence in regard to the rôle of the true and the beautiful in life. Material progress relates to the creation of a greater abundance in the basic necessities of human life, fuller access of the masses to such abundance, and increased security in livelihood. It also encompasses growing physical security in the way of lessening the dangers of war and the physical destruction associated therewith.

If progress is to be well-rounded and assured there must be improvement in all these fields of human well-being—in the totality of human experience. The growth of knowledge cannot assure progress if the increased information is used to achieve the destruction of the human race and all its works more surely and more rapidly. Aesthetic progress accomplishes little if the achievements here are wiped out by war and poverty. And greater productive efficiency is no guarantee of progress if the net result is the impoverishment of the majority and the ultimate disintegration of the whole economic order.

II. THE FALL OF MAN, THE GOLDEN AGE, AND CYCLES OF HISTORY

Far and away the greater part of human history passed without any conscious doctrine of progress to inspire and guide human efforts. The idea of progress really begins with Francis Bacon and the rise of the scientific spirit early in the seventeenth century.

In ancient times, both the Jews and the Gentile nations had little conception of any progress in human experience. The Jews and the Greeks and Romans looked back to perfection in the past—the Jews to the condition in Eden before the Fall of Man, and the Greeks and Romans to an alleged Golden Age. Both the Jews and the classical peoples believed that mankind had declined in the centuries which separated them from Eden and the Golden Age.

While the idea of a decline from better days dominated the thinkers of the ancient world, the Greek and Roman philosophers were also attracted by the conception of cycles of historical development. They contended that civilizations and institutions tend to rise, grow, flourish, decline, and then return to the original starting-point. For example, political institutions may start with a monarchy which passes into tyranny; tyranny gives rise to rebellion which produces aristocracy; but aristocracy descends into oligarchy which, in turn, is followed by democracy; this leads to anarchy and the people turn in desperation once more to monarchy, and the whole cycle is then repeated.

III. THE ORIGINS OF THE IDEA OF PROGRESS

About the only glimmer of an idea of progress in antiquity appeared in the Messianic hope which the Jews appear to have derived from the Egyptian social philosophers. But even the Messiah was hardly expected to be able to do more than restore past glories. The Christians took over the Jewish Messianic conception, of which Jesus was held to be the true embodiment. But the blessed state to which the Christians aspired lay in the City of God of the world to come. Christianity was only incidentally interested in the improvement of earthly conditions. It looked forward to a blessed immortality rather than to an earthly paradise.

The faint beginnings of a notion of progress first appear in the idea of an analogy between the individual organism and society, a conception which we find in the writings of Plato, and was revived in medieval times in the writings of John of Salisbury, Marsiglio of Padua, and Cusanus. Two important writers applied this conception to the growth of civilization: the Muslim historian, Ibn Khaldun (1322–1405), and the French publicist, Jean Bodin (1530–1596). They held that the processes of historic growth are comparable to the life of the individual organism—birth, growth, maturity, decline and death. It is obvious that such an idea was a very qualified conception of progress, for it implied the ultimate decline and disappearance of every society or civilization. There was no unilateral, universal, or unlimited progress envisaged.

The real emergence of the idea of progress must be sought in the rise of the scientific philosophy with such writers as Francis Bacon (1561–1626) and René Descartes (1596–1650). Both Bacon and Descartes believed that the lot of mankind could be greatly and perpetually improved by the application of science to human affairs. Along with Blaise Pascal and William Wotton, Bacon and Descartes ridiculed the conventional notion that the further we go back in time the wiser people were. It is with a disciple of Descartes, Bernard de Fontenelle (1657–1757), that we associate the first comprehensive statement of a theory of progress. He held that, biologically, the ancients and moderns are essentially the same and equal. In the realm of material culture, development has been cumulative and here we have real and spectacular progress. In literature and the arts there is no law of progress and the ancients equalled the moderns. Unreasoning adulation of the ancients is a chief barrier to progress. Charles Perrault (1628–1703) offered a very similar conception of progress. The Abbé St. Pierre (1658–1743) was one of the very first to hold that man could consciously plan out a better future through applying social science to human affairs.

The philosophers of the eighteenth-century Enlightenment gave encouragement to the doctrine of progress. Turgot (1727–1781) stressed the continuity and cumulative nature of progress and looked to future perfection. The most striking statement of the notion of progress by the Rationalists was that set forth by the Marquis de Condorcet (1743–1794). In his *Sketch of the Historical Progress of Mankind* he outlined nine great epochs of human development in the past and maintained that science, rationalism and revolutionary politics would usher in a tenth epoch of unparalleled prosperity, tolerance and enlightenment. Probably the most exuberant prediction of progress and utopia to be achieved through rationality was embodied in the *Enquiry Concerning Political Justice* by William Godwin (1756–1836).

The reaction against the French Revolution and reform through Reason produced a whole school of social philosophers and philosophers of history known as the Romanticists, of whom the more famous were Kant, Herder, Fichte, Schelling, Schlegel, Cousin, Quinet and Laurent. They denied the potency of Reason and attacked the notion of progress through revolutionary legislation. They emphasized the continuity of social and institutional development and substituted the hand of God for Reason as the main factor in the progress of humanity. Hegel worked out a famous formula of progress in his historical dialectic of thesis, antithesis and synthesis.

IV. LEADING IDEAS OF PROGRESS IN THE NINETEENTH CENTURY

The main development in the idea of progress in the nineteenth century consisted in the growth of the concept of determinism in historical development and in the suggestion of laws governing this determinism. Claude Henri de Saint-Simon (1760–1825) and Auguste Comte (1798–1857), the founders of sociology, put forward specific laws of social progress. Comte held that mankind had already passed through two great stages: the theological-military and the metaphysical-legalistic, and was emerging into the scientific-industrial period. Comte also believed that man could plan a social utopia, and offered his own program for so doing.

The rise of the doctrine of evolution gave a great impetus to the notion of progress. The great evolutionary philosopher of the century was Herbert Spencer (1820–1903), whose evolutionary system was based primarily upon physical determinism. Spencer held that social evolution is automatic and inevitable and that we will only retard progress by any man-made plans for social progress. This view was vigorously upheld in the United States by Spencer's American disciple, William Graham Sumner of Yale University. Charles Darwin offered a theory of biological evolution through the struggle for existence and natural selection, but he did not carry over his doctrine into social evolution. This was done by a group of sociologists, led by the Polish writer, Ludwig Gumplowicz. They contended that war among human societies plays the same rôle in social evolution that the struggle for existence does in the biological realm. This hypothesis was assailed by the Russian sociologist and internationalist, Jacques Novicow. The most scientific effort to apply Darwinian views to the social realm was contained in the book on *Societal Evolution* (1915) by Sumner's disciple, Albert Galloway Keller. The most famous adoption of evolutionary conceptions to explain the rise and development of early institutions was embodied in the vastly influential work of Lewis Henry Morgan, *Ancient Society* (1877).

For the most part, the evolutionary philosophy of the nineteenth century, as applied to human affairs, favored the notion that social progress is automatic and that man will only impede advances by his bungling plans of reform. This conception was challenged by a man who was both a great biologist and a great sociologist, Lester F. Ward (1841–1913). He maintained that, while progress has been automatic in the past, though wasteful and brutal, the growth of social science is enabling man to plan out his social future scientifically and thus vastly accelerate the rate of progress and reduce the social wastage associated with spontaneous progress through social selection. Ward's views were also shared by other eminent sociologists such as Albion W. Small, Ludwig Stein, Leonard T. Hobhouse, and C. A. Ellwood. Such men were the fathers of the notion of progress through social planning.

Next to evolutionary philosophy the most influential contribution to the idea of progress during the nineteenth century was the development of Marxian Socialism and its associated materialistic philosophy of history. Marx held that social progress is automatic and inevitable and that material factors, technological and economic, control the nature and rate of social progress. He maintained that economic institutions determine the character of social, political, legal, religious and ethical development. The present capitalistic era is to be displaced by the emergence of the socialist era based upon the dominion of the working proletariat and upon production for use rather than for private profit. The main dynamic factor which will produce this transition from capitalism to socialism is the "class-struggle" between capitalistic exploiters and workers. Marxism, with certain qualifications dictated by circumstances, was put into actual operation in Soviet Russia after 1917.

V. SUBSTITUTION OF THE NOTION OF SOCIAL CHANGE FOR THE IDEA OF PROGRESS

The events of the twentieth century have had a decidedly chastening effect upon the nineteenth-century optimism with respect to inevitable progress. The impressive development of machinery, with the possibility of providing an abundance for all, has been actually associated with serious economic depressions which put millions in the breadlines. Capitalism was seriously undermined in the Old World at the very time when its technological basis was being improved by leaps and bounds. The attainment of democracy was not accompanied by greater political purity or efficiency and the masses failed to take an active and intelligent interest in politics. World wars wasted the substance of nations, killed off millions, wiped out historic monuments and works of art, and reduced whole nations to mob hysteria and the ethics of the lynching bee. The appearance of the atom bomb in 1945 pointed up the menace of war to any assured progress and security. The development of science and technology, long regarded as the most evident and obvious proof of progress, could not well be held to foster progress if the net result was economic collapse and devastating world wars.

Therefore, writers on the subject have tended to abandon the idea of progress, which implied wholesale advance on all social fronts, and have come to substitute for this the conception of *social change*. If the ultimate destruction of civilization through war and economic chaos is a stark prospect in our century, then it is difficult indeed to sustain the thesis of substantial and comprehensive human progress, whatever the advances in some particular phases of our culture. But social change can be proved. Even the atomic bomb and its consequences constitute change, though it may be a calamity which will doom humanity. So, as of the date of the writing of this chapter, few discerning writers any longer dogmatically assert the reality of total human progress. They point out many sweeping social changes but await future developments before they can decide whether or not the historical experience of mankind gives evidence of true and sustained progress.

This modification of attitude towards progress has been reflected in a number of pessimistic theories of history, anticipated in the late nineteenth century by the Adams brothers, Brooks and Henry, and most completely expressed in the books of Oswald Spengler, Arnold J. Toynbee and Pitirim Sorokin. We have reviewed this literature in a preceding chapter and need not repeat the material in this place.

This literary pessimism has been paralleled by a marked increase of flight into dogmatic and mystical cults similar to that which was witnessed with the downfall of Greek and Roman civilization in the fourth and fifth centuries. Indeed, there is much evidence of the same "failure of nerve," which Gilbert Murray regarded as the most characteristic intellectual and moral trait of the decline of classical civilization. Even some formerly tough-minded sceptics, like C. E. M. Joad, have succumbed.

Therefore, we are brought to the same final conclusion as in the preceding chapter, namely, that the outcome depends upon whether or not we are able to bring our institutions up to date and master the problems of our atomic age. On July 1, 1946, *Time Magazine* quoted a striking paragraph from the *Journal* of the de Goncourt brothers, written in 1870:

They were saying that Berthelot had predicted that a hundred years from now, thanks to physical and chemical science, men would know of what the atom is constituted. . . . To all of this we raise no objection, but we have a feeling that, when this time comes in science, God with his white beard will come down to earth, swinging a bunch of keys, and will say to humanity, the way they say at 5 o'clock in the Salon: "Closing time, gentlemen."

There is all too much evidence that such may well be the case. But no such dire outcome is necessary or inevitable. The difference between the discovery and application of intra-atomic energy and preceding scientific and technological discoveries is one of degree only. If atomic energy and all other scientific and mechanical aids to mankind can be used for peaceful purposes and for greater production for human use, an unparalleled and scarcely dreamed-of era of prosperity, security, leisure and happiness may lie ahead for humanity. But, this time, social institutions must actually catch up with the scientific and mechanical procession—and that fairly rapidly—or all of them seem destined to go down together in a common and universal ruin.

---

1. On the idea of progress, see: J. B. Bury, *The Idea of Progress* (New York: Macmillan, 1932); A. G. Keller, *Societal Evolution* (New York: Macmillan, 1931); W. F. Ogburn, *Social Change* (New York: Viking, 1922); J. S. Schapiro, *Condorcet* (New York: Harcourt, 1934); F. J. Teggart, ed., *The Idea of Progress* (Berkeley: University of California Press, 1925); A. J. Todd, *Theories of Social Progress* (New York: Macmillan, 1918); W. D. Wallis, *Culture and Progress* (New York: McGraw-Hill, 1930).

SELECTED BIBLIOGRAPHY

H. E. Barnes, *Sociology and Political Theory* (New York: Knopf, 1924). Survey of sociological writings on political problems. Contains material on sociological contributions to political origins.

————, *The New History and the Social Studies* (New York: Century, 1925). Reviews sociological and anthropological contributions to the history of human society.

————, *Psychology and History* (New York: Century, 1925). Deals with psychological and cultural analysis of social origins and cultural development.

————, *The History and Prospects of the Social Sciences* (New York: Knopf, 1925). Comprehensive symposium on the development of the social sciences. Chapters on History, Anthropology, Sociology and Jurisprudence are especially relevant to the subject-matter of this book.

————, *History of Historical Writing* (Norman: University of Oklahoma Press, 1937). Gives much material on relations of history and historical sociology.

————, *An Introduction to the History of Sociology* (Chicago: University of Chicago Press, 1947). Contains chapters by experts on the leading historical sociologists.

————, and Howard Becker, *Social Thought from Lore to Science* (Boston: Heath, 1938). Comprehensive work, covering, incidentally, all the leading writers on historical sociology and related subjects from ancient to contemporary times.

————, and Howard Becker, *Contemporary Social Theory* (New York: Century, 1940). Collaborative work, with many chapters bearing on historical sociology and a special chapter on that subject by Becker.

————, *Social Institutions* (New York: Prentice-Hall, 1942). Most complete panorama of cultural lag and institutional maladjustment.

L. L. Bernard, *The Field and Methods of Sociology* (New York: Long and Smith, 1924). Symposium on all fields of sociology, with a chapter on Historical Sociology, by Howard Becker.

Franz Boas, *Race, Language and Culture* (New York: Macmillan, 1940). Summary of main theoretical views of the leader of critical American anthropology.

180

E. S. Bogardus, *A History of Social Thought* (Los Angeles: Miller, 1928). Broad general survey of the whole history of social thought.

J. B. Bury, *The Idea of Progress* (New York: Macmillan, 1932). Standard work on history of theories of progress.

L. M. Bristol, *Social Adaptation* (Cambridge: Harvard University Press, 1915). Review of selected fields of contemporary social thought. Has much material on Social Darwinism, its critique, and related topics.

F. Stuart Chapin, *Cultural Change* (New York: Century, 1928). Important sociological summary of the methods and materials of historical and cultural sociology.

R. B. Dixon, *The Building of Cultures* (New York: Scribner, 1928). Survey and analysis of theories of cultural and institutional development, with special stress on diffusion.

C. A. Ellwood, *The Story of Social Philosophy* (New York: Prentice-Hall, 1938). Readable survey of the evolution of social thought.

————, *Cultural Evolution* (New York: Century, 1927). Pioneer work by sociologist on historical and cultural sociology.

Alexander Goldenweiser, *History, Psychology and Culture* (New York: Knopf, 1933). Contains many valuable critical essays on theories of cultural and institutional development.

A. C. Haddon, *History of Anthropology* (New York: Putnam, 1910). Brief pioneer work on origin and development of anthropology, archeology and historical sociology.

E. C. Hayes, *Recent Developments in the Social Sciences* (Philadelphia: Lippincott, 1927). Symposium, with chapters on recent trends in sociology, anthropology and history.

F. N. House, *The Range of Social Theory* (New York: Holt, 1929). Topical review of sociological theories bearing on various aspects of social and institutional life. Contains much material related to historical sociology.

————, *The Development of Sociology* (New York: McGraw-Hill, 1936). Very readable survey of contemporary sociological theories.

J. P. Lichtenberger, *Development of Social Theory* (New York: Century, 1923). General review of the development of social thought. Chapters on Comte, Spencer and Social Darwinism are the most valuable for the purposes of this book.

R. H. Lowie, *The History of Ethnological Theory* (New York: Farrar and Rinehart, 1937). Invaluable, clear and authoritative summary of the development and nature of anthropological theories and achievements.

G. A. Lundberg, Read Bain and Nels Anderson, *Trends in American*

Sociology (New York: Harpers, 1929). Symposium, in which the most important chapters for historical sociology are those on the theories of sociology and culture.

C. E. Merriam and H. E. Barnes, *Political Theories: Recent Times* (New York: Macmillan, 1924). Collaborative work, containing important chapters on political origins, and race and history.

W. F. Ogburn, *Social Change* (New York: Huebsch, 1922). Pioneer work on cultural lag.

————, and Alexander Goldenweiser, *The Social Sciences* (Boston: Houghton Mifflin, 1927). Symposium containing relevant chapters on sociology, anthropology and history.

Paul Radin, *The Method and Theory of Ethnology* (New York: McGraw-Hill, 1933). Good example of anthropological defense of extreme Historicism.

Wilhelm Schmidt, *The Culture Historical Method of Ethnology* (New York: Fortuny's 1939). Able survey and critique of anthropological theories by a leading European diffusionist.

A. W. Small, *Origins of Sociology* (Chicago: University of Chicago Press, 1924). Contains much material on the relation of history and historical theories to the origins of modern sociology.

Pitirim Sorokin, *Contemporary Sociological Theories* (New York: Harper, 1928). Very erudite encyclopedia of contemporary social theory. Especially notable for covering of technical and obscure materials not usually found in other books of this kind.

B. J. Stern, *Lewis Henry Morgan: Social Evolutionist* (Chicago: University of Chicago Press, 1931). Brief survey of the life and work of the most important figure in the establishment of historical sociology. Should be compared with the chapter on Morgan by L. A. White in Barnes, *et al., Introduction to the History of Sociology.*

A. J. Todd, *Theories of Social Progress* (New York: Macmillan, 1918). Useful review of doctrines. Conventional in tone.

W. D. Wallis, *Culture and Progress* (New York: McGraw-Hill, 1930). Elaborate review of the theories and factors of social progress and cultural change.

L. A. White, "The Expansion of the Scope of Science," *Journal of the Washington Academy of Sciences,* XXXVII (June 15, 1947), pp. 181–210. Able argument for an independent science of culturology.

Clark Wissler, *Man and Culture* (New York: Crowell, 1923). Survey of the main processes and fields of cultural growth by a leading American anthropologist.

INDEX